The Art of
Creative
Thinking

The Art of
Creative
Thinking

How to be innovative and
develop great ideas

JOHN ADAIR

**KOGAN
PAGE**

London and Philadelphia

Publisher's note

Every possible effort has been made to ensure that the information contained in this book is accurate at the time of going to press, and the publishers and authors cannot accept responsibility for any errors or omissions, however caused. No responsibility for loss or damage occasioned to any person acting, or refraining from action, as a result of the material in this publication can be accepted by the editor, the publisher or the author.

First published in Great Britain in 1990 by the Talbot Adair Press
This edition published in Great Britain and the United States by Kogan Page Limited in 2007
First published in paperback in 2009
Reprinted 2009

Kogan Page Limited
120 Pentonville Road
London N1 9JN
United Kingdom
www.koganpage.com

Kogan Page US
525 South 4th Street, #241
Philadelphia PA 19147
USA

© John Adair, 1990, 2007, 2009

ISBN 978 0 7494 5483 8

British Library Cataloguing-in-Publication Data

A CIP record for this book is available from the British Library.

Library of Congress Cataloging-in-Publication Data

Adair, John Eric, 1934–
   The art of creative thinking : how to be innovative and develop great ideas / John Adair. -- Pbk. ed.
       p. cm. -- (The John Adair leadership library)
   Originally published: London : Philadelphia : Kogan Page, 2007.
   Includes index.
   ISBN 978-0-7494-5483-8
   1. Creative thinking. I. Title.
   BF408.A28 2009
   153.3'5--dc22
                                                                            2008043882

Typeset by Jean Cussons Typesetting, Diss, Norfolk
Printed and bound in Great Britain by MPG Books Ltd, Bodmin, Cornwall

Contents

About the author

John Adair is widely regarded as the world's leading authority on leadership and leadership development. Over a million managers worldwide have taken part in the Action-Centred Leadership programmes he pioneered.

From St Paul's School, London, John won a scholarship to Cambridge University. He holds the higher degrees of Master of Letters from Oxford University and Doctor of Philosophy from King's College London, and he is also a Fellow of the Royal Historical Society. Recently the People's Republic of China awarded him the title of Honorary Professor in recognition of his 'outstanding research and contribution in the field of Leadership'.

John had a colourful early career. He served as a platoon commander in the Scots Guards in Egypt, and then became the only national serviceman to serve in the Arab Legion, where he became adjutant of a Bedouin regiment. He was virtually in command of the garrison of Jerusalem and was in the front line for six weeks. After national service he qualified as a deckhand and sailed an Arctic trawler to Iceland. He then worked as a hospital orderly in the operating theatre of a hospital.

After being senior lecturer in military history and adviser in leadership training at the Royal Military Academy Sandhurst, and Associate Director of The Industrial Society, in 1979 John became the world's first Professor of Leadership Studies at the University of Surrey.

Between 1981 and 1986 John worked with Sir John Harvey-Jones at ICI, introducing a leadership development strategy that helped to change the loss-making, bureaucratic giant into the first British company to make a billion pounds profit.

John has written over 50 books, now in 25 languages. Recent titles published by Kogan Page include *Leadership and Motivation*, *Develop Your Leadership Skills*, *Leadership for Innovation* and *Decision Making and Problem Solving Strategies*. Apart from being an author, he is also a teacher and consultant, advising many organizations in business, government, education, health and the voluntary sector.

Introduction

Dust as we are, the immortal spirit grows
Like harmony in music; there is a dark
Inscrutable workmanship that reconciles
Discordant elements, makes them cling together
In one society.

William Wordsworth

The importance of creative thinking today needs no emphasis. In your profession or sphere of work you will have a competitive advantage if you develop your ability to come up with new ideas. In your personal life, too, creative thinking can lead you into new paths of creative activity. It can enrich your life – though not always in the way you expect.

There have been many books on creativity and creative thinking. What is distinctive about this one? My new concept is that of the Depth Mind (see Chapter 13). Of course, the reality behind it – the creative activity of the unconscious mind – is not by any means new. My contribution, however, is to present that reality in a fresh way. I have also put it into context within a simple framework of mental activity: the *analysing, synthesizing* and *valuing* functions of the mind when it is thinking to some purpose. Oddly enough, no one has done that before.

This is not simply a book about creative thinking. Its aim is to help you in practical ways to become a more creative thinker. Being essentially a practical sort of book, it does not go into the philosophy or psychology of creativity in any depth, except as far as these disciplines have thrown up valuable insights or tips for practical creative thinkers.

Nor have I explored here what might be called the organizational dimension of the subject. How do organizations foster or stifle creative thinking? Why are some organizations better than others at introducing changes and implementing them? My companion book to this one, *Leadership for Innovation*, addresses those questions. For how new ideas are brought to market in the shape of products or services is another subject. My focus here is upon you as an individual creative thinker, regardless of where you are employed.

Each chapter has one simple core idea – something fairly tangible or well-attested. Depending on its nature, I then briefly develop and illustrate it. Then I summarize the discussion in some simple keypoints. These are not merely summaries, however, for sometimes new thoughts are introduced in them.

It follows that there is really no logical order to the book. Creative thinking cannot be reduced to a set of sequential steps. Imagine the chapters as being spokes of a wheel or pieces of amber hung on a necklace. So you do not necessarily have to start at the beginning – find a chapter that interests you and work outwards. I hope that you find this book stimulating and enjoyable as well as instructive. May it take you forward on your journey as a creative thinker.

Among other things, these pages will help you to:

- develop your understanding of the creative process;

- overcome barriers or blocks to having new ideas;

- enlarge your parameters of vision;

- learn to build on ideas as well as criticize them;

- increase your tolerance for uncertainty and doubt;

- listen, look and read with a creative attitude;

- make time to think;

- become more confident in yourself as a creative person.

1

On human creativity

To create is always to do something new.

Martin Luther

Imagine for a moment that an unknown animal had been discovered deep in the jungles of South America. It is destined to replace the dog and the cat in popularity as a domestic pet during this century. What does it look like? What are its winning characteristics? Take some paper now and draw it, making some notes about your sketch.

Your new animal may have short silky fur like a mole. Its face may be borrowed from a koala bear and its round cuddly body from a wombat. It is blue in colour and green in temperament, for it does not foul the pavements or parks. That sounds a bit like a cat. It repels unwanted intruders more effectively than a guard-dog, but is as gentle with children as a white rabbit.

What you are tending to do, consciously or subconsciously, is to borrow characteristics from the animals you know. There is nothing wrong with that. For we humans cannot make anything out of nothing. Once, a distinguished visitor to Henry Ford's auto plants met him after an exhaustive tour of the factory. The visitor was lost in wonder and admiration. 'It seems almost impossible, Mr Ford,' he told the industrialist, 'that a man, starting 25 years ago with practically nothing, could accomplish all this.' Ford replied, 'But that's hardly correct. Every man starts with all there is. Everything is here – the essence and substance of all there is.' The potential materials – the elements, constituents or substances of which something can be made or composed – are all here in our universe.

You may have noticed that we tend to bestow the word creative on products that are very far removed from the original raw materials used. A masterpiece by Rubens was once a collection of blue, red, yellow and green worms of paint on the artist's palette. Now the physical materials – paints and canvas for an artist, paper and pen for an author – are entirely secondary. Creation here is more in the mind. Perception, ideas and feelings are combined in a concept or vision. Of course, the artist, writer or composer needs skill and technique to form on canvas or paper what is conceived in the mind.

The same principle holds good in creative thinking as in creativity in general. Our creative imaginations must have something to work on. We do not form new ideas out of nothing. As Henry Ford said above, the raw materials are all there. The creative mind sees possibilities in them or connections that are invisible to less creative minds.

That conclusion brings enormous relief. You do not have to conjure up new ideas from the air. Your task as a creative thinker is to combine ideas or elements that already exist. If the result is an unlikely but valuable combination of ideas or things that hitherto were not thought to be linked, then you will be seen as a creative thinker. You will have added value to the synthesis, for a whole is more than the sum of its parts.

KEYPOINTS

▣ With creativity we start with what already exists.

▣ We recognize creativity where the artist or thinker of genius has transformed the materials at hand into a new creation of enduring value.

▣ 'He is most original who adapts from the most sources', as the saying goes. You will be creative when you start seeing or making connections between ideas that appear to others to be far apart: the wider the apparent distance the greater the degree of creative thinking involved.

▣ Creativity is the faculty of mind and spirit that enables us to bring into existence, ostensibly out of nothing, something of use, order, beauty or significance.

No matter how old you get, if you can keep the desire to be creative, you're keeping the child in you alive.

Anon

2

Use the stepping stones of analogy

I invent nothing; I rediscover.

Rodin

Put yourself into the shoes of an inventor. You have become dissatisfied with the solution to some existing problem or daily necessity. You are casting about in your mind for a new idea. Something occurs to you, possibly suggested by reading about other people's attempts in the files of the patent office. You go home and sketch your invention, and then make a model of it.

There are other later stages, of course, but let us stop here. The point is that the model you have reached may well have been suggested by an analogy from nature. Indeed you could look upon nature as a storehouse of models waiting to be used by inventors. In the box below is a quiz, which you might like to attempt to answer now:

QUIZ

List specific inventions that were (or might have been) suggested to creative thinkers by the following natural phenomena:

1. human arms

2. cats

3. seagulls

4. a frozen salmon

5. spiders

6. earthworms

7. a flower

8. the eye of a fly

9. conical shells

10. animal bone structures

Can you add to that list? Take a piece of paper and see if you can add at least five other inventions that have sprung into the inventor's mind by using an analogy as a stepping stone.

In case you get stuck, here are some more natural phenomena that could have suggested inventions to alert creative thinkers. Can you identify what these inventions might have been?

11. dew drops on leaves

12. human skulls

13. bamboo

14. human foot

15. human lungs

16. larynx

Answers on page 125–27, in Appendix C at the back of the book.

Remember that what the natural model suggests is usually a principle that nature has evolved or employed to solve a particular problem or necessity in a given situation. That principle can be extracted like venom from a snake and applied to solve a human problem. Radar, for example, came from studying the uses of reflected sound waves from bats. The way a clam shell opens suggested the design for aircraft cargo doors. The built-in system weakness of the pea pod suggested a way of opening cigarette packages, a method now widely used in the packaging industry.

The same fundamental principle – that models for the solution to our problems probably already exist, we do not have to create them from nothing – can be applied to all creative thinking, not just to inventing new products. Take human organization for example. Most of the principles involved can be found in nature: hierarchy (baboons), division of labour (ants, bees), networks (spiders' webs), and so on. If you are trying to create a new organization you will find plenty of ready-made models in human society, past or present. Remember, however, that these are only analogies. If you copy directly you are heading for trouble. More of that later.

Nor are we limited to nature for the kind of metaphors or analogies that trigger creative thinking. Soichiro Honda was an engineer who excelled in creative thinking and innovation. While he was building his first four-cylinder motorcycle he gradually realized that although the engine was fine his designers had made the machine look squat and ugly. He decided to take a week's break in Kyoto. One day, sitting in an ancient temple, he found himself fascinated by the face of a statue of the Buddha. He felt that he could see a resemblance between the look of Buddha's face and how he imagined the front of the motorbike would be. Having spent the rest of the week studying other statues of the Buddha in Kyoto he returned and worked with the designers on a harmonious style that reflected something of the beauty he had glimpsed.

KEYPOINTS

▓ Thinking by analogy, or analogizing, plays a key part in imaginative thinking. This is especially so when it comes to creative thinking.

▓ Nature suggests models and principles for the solutions of problems.

▓ There are other models or analogies to be found in existing products and organizations. Why reinvent the principle of the wheel when it has already been discovered? Some simple research may save you the bother of thinking it out for yourself.

▓ Honda's story illustrates a principle that we shall explore more fully in Chapter 4. He had a wide span of analogy – who else would have seen an analogy between a Buddha's smile and the front of a motorcycle?

Everything has been thought of before, but the problem is to think of it again.

Goethe

3

Make the strange familiar and the familiar strange

Discovery consists of seeing what everyone has seen and thinking what nobody has thought.

Anon

When primitive natives in New Guinea saw an aircraft for the first time they called it 'the big bird'. Birds were familiar to them. Their first step towards comprehending something totally strange or unfamiliar to them was to assume it was an unusual example of something already known to them. We assimilate the strange or unfamiliar by comparing it consciously or unconsciously to what is familiar to us.

With further experience the natives doubtless discovered that in some respects aircraft are like birds and in some respects they are not. In other words, following the 'big bird' hypothesis, noting the point where it begins to break down, is a useful way of exploring and beginning to understand a new phenomenon. Therefore you should use analogy to explore and understand what seems to be strange.

Not so long ago I conducted a seminar on leadership for heads of university departments. Leadership and management – and the difference between them – were quite new concepts for many of the participants. One of them, a professor of chemistry, used the familiar to understand the unfamiliar in this way:

> In chemistry a reaction between two compounds that can react is often put down in notation as follows:
>
> $A + B \leftrightarrows AB$
>
> Many reactions proceed slowly, if at all, without a catalyst. This to my mind is the role of leadership in getting a job done – to catalyse the process.
>
> There are various ways in which the analogy could be amplified but if you consider a rough equation of
>
> PROBLEM $\leftrightarrows$ SOLUTION
>
> management will realize a solution in many instances but leadership will usually catalyse it. There is a little magic involved!

Creative thinking often involves a leap in the dark. You are looking for something new. By definition, if it is really novel, neither you nor anyone else will have had that idea. Often you cannot get there in one jump. If you can hit upon an analogy of what the unknown idea may be like you are halfway there.

The reverse process – making the familiar strange – is equally useful to the creative thinker. Familiarity breeds conformity. Because things, ideas or people are familiar we stop thinking about them. As Seneca said, 'Familiarity reduces the greatness of things.' Seeing them as strange, odd, problematic, unsatisfactory or only half-known restarts the engines of your minds. Remember the saying that God hides things from us by putting them near to us.

As an exercise in warming up your latent powers of creative thinking you can do no better than to apply this principle of making the familiar strange. Take something that you frequently see or experience, or perhaps an everyday occurrence like the sun rising or the rain falling. Set aside half an hour with some paper and a pen or pencil. Reflect or meditate on the object, concentrating on what you do not know about it.

A member of your family or a friend makes a good subject for this exercise. When we say we know someone we usually mean that we have a hazy notion of their likes and dislikes, together with a rough idea of their personality or temperament. We believe we can predict more or less accurately how the person will react. We think we know when our relative or friend is deviating from their normal behaviour. But take yourself as an analogy. Does anyone know everything about you? Could you in all honesty say that you fully know yourself?

'We do not know people – their concerns, their loves and hates, their thoughts', said the late novelist Iris Murdoch in a television interview. 'For me the people I see around me every day are more extraordinary than any characters in my books.' The implication is that below the surface of familiarity there is a wonderful unknown world to be explored.

KEYPOINTS

▪ The process of understanding anything or anyone unfamiliar, foreign, unnatural, unaccountable – what is not already known, heard or seen – is best begun by relating it by analogy to what we know already. But it should not end there.

▪ The reverse process of making the familiar strange is equally important for creative thinking. We do not think about what we know. Here artists can help us to become aware of the new within the old.

▪ 'No man really knows about other human beings,' wrote John Steinbeck, 'the best he can do is to suppose that they are like himself.'

▪ 'Last night I thought over a thousand plans, but this morning I went my old way', says the Chinese proverb. Settled habits of thought, over-addiction to the familiar, will smother the dreams and ideas of the night.

▪ This morning you made a cup of tea or coffee and had your breakfast – the same as yesterday. But was it? You will never even brush your teeth in precisely the same way as yesterday. Every minute is unique.

The essence of the creative act is to see the familiar as strange.

Anon

4

Widen your span of relevance

To perceive things in the germ is intelligence.

Lao-Tzu

Farming in his native Berkshire in the early eighteenth century, the British agriculturalist, Jethro Tull, developed a drill enabling seeds to be sown mechanically, and so spaced that cultivation between rows was possible in the growth period. Tull was an organist, and it was the principle of the organ that gave him his new idea. What he was doing, in effect, was to transfer the technical means of achieving a practical purpose from one field to another.

The essential ingredients of the story are as follows. Tull was confronted with a problem and dissatisfied with the existing solutions to it. Suddenly a spark jumped between the problem and his knowledge of another technology. He found a model or analogy. Then it was a question of applying the principle and developing the technology to the new task in hand. The less obvious the connection between the two fields the more we are likely to call it creative thinking.

Therefore it is not surprising that inventors and other creative thinkers have knowledge in more than one field. They may even work in a quite different sphere from the one in which they make their names as discoverers or inventors. Compare the following list of inventions in the box below with the occupations of their inventors:

Invention	*Inventor's main occupation*
Ballpoint pen	Sculptor
Safety razor	Traveller in corks
Kodachrome films	Musician
Automatic telephone	Undertaker
Parking meter	Journalist
Pneumatic tyre	Veterinary surgeon
Long-playing record	Television engineer

The lack of expert or specialized knowledge in a given field is no bar to being able to make a creative contribution. Indeed, too much knowledge may be a disadvantage. As Disraeli said, we must 'learn to unlearn'. Sir Barnes Wallis, the British aeronautical engineer who helped to develop the Concorde supersonic airliner and the swing-wing aircraft, failed his London matriculation examination at the age of 16. 'I knew nothing,' he said in a television interview, 'except how to think, how to grapple with a problem and then go on grappling with it until you had solved it.'

When you are grappling with a problem remember to *widen your span of relevance*. Look at the technologies available in fields other than your own, possibly in those that may appear to others to be so far removed as to be irrelevant. They may give you a clue.

'Experience has shown,' wrote Edgar Allan Poe, 'and a true philosophy will always show, that a vast, perhaps the larger, portion of the truth arises from the seemingly irrelevant.'

That is a great reason for travelling. For one seeing is worth 100 hearings. Go and look for yourself. You may discover technologies that are ripe for transfer. It has been said that as individuals the Japanese are not highly rated as creative thinkers, but in groups they are much more creative. The secret of the Japanese economic miracle is that they travelled the world in search of the latest technologies that they could transfer to Japan, there to be endlessly adapted and improved. Quality Circles, for example, was a system for getting work people to think creatively about their products or services, which made its first appearance in the United States after World War II. The Japanese transferred that system and developed it with outstanding success into their own industry.

KEYPOINTS

▪ The transfer of technology from one field to another, usually with some degree of alteration and adaptation, is one way in which you can make a creative contribution.

▪ You may be familiar with a body of knowledge or technical capability unknown to others in your field because you have worked in more than one industry. Or it may come about as a result of your travels to other countries.

▪ People with a narrow span of relevance are thinking within the tramlines and boundaries of their own industry. Leap over the wall! Develop a wide span of relevance, for there are connections between every other industry in the world and yours – if only you could see them.

▪ It comes down to your 'power to connect the seemingly unconnected', or at least the things that hitherto have not been brought together in a new and interesting relation.

It is the function of creative people to perceive the relations between thoughts, or things or forms of expression that may seem utterly different, and to combine them into some new forms – the power to connect the seemingly unconnected.

William Plomer

5

Practise serendipity

The real magic of discovery lies not in seeking new land-scapes but in having new eyes.

Marcel Proust

Serendipity is a happy word. Horace Walpole coined it to denote the faculty of making unexpected and delightful discoveries by accident. In a letter to a friend (28 January 1754) he says that he formed it from the title of a fairy story, *The Three Princes of Serendip* (an ancient name for Sri Lanka), for the princes 'were always making discoveries, by accidents and sagacity, of things they were not in quest of'.

If serendipity suggests chance – the finding of things of value when we are not actually looking for them – the finder must at least be able to see the creative possibilities of his or her discovery. Edison was seeking something else when he came across the idea of the mimeograph. He had the good sense to realize that he had made a discovery of importance and soon found a use for it.

Serendipity goes against the grain of narrow focus thinking, where you concentrate your mind upon an objective or goal to the exclusion of all else. It invites you to have a wide span of attention, wide enough to notice something of significance even though it is apparently irrelevant or useless to you at present.

The three princes in the story were travellers. Explorers into the unknown often make unexpected discoveries. As the proverbial schoolboy or girl knows, Christopher Columbus was seeking a new sea route to Asia when he discovered the New World. He thought he had reached India, which is why he called the natives he found there Indians. When you travel you should do so in a serendipitous frame of mind. Expect the unexpected. You may not discover America but you will have some happy and unexpected 'finds'.

'Thinking will always give you a reward, though not always what you expected.' These wise words were spoken by the Canadian entrepreneur and businessman Lord Roy Thomson of Fleet.

When you are thinking you are travelling mentally, you are on a journey. For genuine thinking is always a process possessing direction. Look out for the unexpected thoughts, however lightly they stir in your mind. Sometimes an unsuspected path or byway of thought that opens up might be more rewarding than following the fixed route you had set yourself.

Christopher Milne once unveiled a bronze statue of Winnie the Pooh, the toy bear that became both the joy and the bane of his life. Milne and his father took the name 'Pooh' from a swan that had died and 'Winnie' from the child-loving black bear that was the mascot of a Canadian regiment that left her in Regent's Park when it went to the front in 1914. A A Milne's literary executives had commissioned the sculpture.

'There are two ways of doing things', said Christopher Milne at the unveiling ceremony. 'You can decide exactly what you want to do and make a list on a piece of paper and then do it all precisely. This was Rabbit's way. At the end everyone says, "Well done, Rabbit. Clever Rabbit." Or you can have a rough idea of what you want, hope to set off in the right direction and probably end up with something quite different. Then you realize it isn't such a bad thing after all. That was Pooh's way and that's how we've done this.'

With hindsight it is often easier to see the effects of serendipity in your life. Looking back, can you identify three occasions when you made important discoveries, or met key people in your life's story, when you were not expecting to do so?

KEYPOINTS

▪ Serendipity means finding valuable and agreeable ideas or things – or people – when you are not consciously seeking them.

▪ You are more likely to be serendipitous if you have a wide span of attention and a broad range of interests.

▪ Being over-organized, planning your life down to the last minute like a control freak, is inimical to creativity. For chaos often breeds ideas. As A A Milne said: 'One of the advantages of being disorderly is that one is constantly making exciting discoveries.'

▪ Developing your capacity for creative thinking will bring you rewards, but they may not be the ones you expect now.

▪ A creative thinker needs to be adventurous and open-minded like a resourceful explorer.

▪ Sometimes in life you never quite know what you are looking for until you find it.

Fortune brings in some boats that are not steered.
William Shakespeare

6

Chance favours only the prepared mind

Where observation is concerned, chance favours only the prepared mind.

Louis Pasteur

Before the development of the float process by a research team led by Sir Alastair Pilkington, glass-making was labour-intensive and time-consuming, mainly because of the need for grinding and polishing surfaces to get a brilliant finish.

Pilkington's proprietary process eliminated this final manufacturing stage by floating the glass, after it is cast from a melting furnace, over a bath of molten tin about the size of a tennis court. The idea for 'rinsing' glass over a molten tin bath came to Sir Alastair when he stood at his kitchen sink washing dishes. The float process gives a distortion-free glass of uniform quality with bright, fire-polished surfaces. Savings in costs are considerable. A float line needs only half the number of workers to produce three times as much glass as old production methods. Since the introduction of the process, it is estimated to have earned Pilkington over $2 billion in royalties.

It is interesting to reflect how many other inventions have been the result of such unexpected or chance occurrences as befell Sir Alastair Pilkington at his kitchen sink. The classic example, of course, is the discovery of penicillin by Sir Alexander Fleming. The sweetening effect of saccharine, another example, was accidentally discovered by a chemist who happened to eat his lunch in the laboratory without washing his hands after some experiments. Ira W Rufel observed the effects when a feeder failed to place a sheet of paper in a lithograph machine, and the work on the printing surface left its full impression upon the printing cylinder: it led him to invent the offset method of printing. The idea of the mirror galvanometer first occurred to William Thompson when he happened to notice a reflection of light from his monocle.

Charles Goodyear discovered the vulcanization of rubber in 1839 by similar observation of a chance event. He had been experimenting for many years to find a process of treating crude or synthetic rubber chemically to give it such useful properties as strength and stability, but without success. One day as he was mixing rubber with sulphur he spilt some of the mixture on to the top of a hot stove. The heat vulcanized it at once. Goodyear immediately saw the solution to the problem that had baffled him for years.

As Goodyear pointed out, however, chance was by no means the only factor in his useful discovery. He said:

> I was for many years seeking to accomplish this object, and *allowing nothing to escape my notice* that related to it. Like the falling apple before Newton's gaze, it was suggestive of an important fact to one whose mind was previously prepared to draw an inference from *any occurrence which might favour the object of his research.* While I admit that these discoveries of mine were not the result of scientific chemical investigation, I am not willing to admit that they are the result of what is commonly called accident. I claim them to be the result of *the closest application and observation.*

I have put some of Goodyear's words into italics because they highlight the importance of having a wide focus of attention and keen powers of observation. His message is admirably summed up in Pasteur's famous words: 'In the field of observation, chance favours only the prepared mind.'

What does it mean for you to have a prepared mind? You have to be purposeful in that you are seeking an answer or solution to some problem. You have become exceptionally sensitive to any occurrence that might be relevant to that search. You have the experience to recognize and interpret a clue when you see or hear one. That entails the ability to remain alert and sensitive for the unexpected while watching for the expected. You will have to be willing to invest a good deal of time in fruitless work, for opportunities in the form of significant clues do not come often. In those long hours, experiment with new procedures. Expose yourself to the maximum extent to the possibility of encountering a fortunate accident.

KEYPOINTS

▪ Things that happen unpredictably, without discerning human intention or observable cause, can be stitched into the process of creative thinking.

▪ Such accidents tend to happen to those who deserve them. Do not wait for them, but learn to watch out for them.

▪ To see and recognize a clue in such unexpected events demands sensitivity and observation.

▪ To interpret the clue and realize its possible significance requires knowledge without preconceptions, imaginative thinking, the habit of reflecting on unexplained observations – and some original flair.

▪ Again, the importance of having an open mind and a degree of curiosity stands out clearly. You have to constantly ask yourself questions about what is happening around you – and be ready for surprising answers.

I have no exceptional talents, other than a passionate curiosity.

Einstein

7

Curiosity

Curiosity is one of the permanent and certain characteristics of a vigorous intellect.

Samuel Johnson

If you or I had been in Napoleon's shoes after his shattering defeat at Waterloo we might well have lapsed into a state of inward-looking depression if not despair. Not so Napoleon. Following his defeat he abdicated with the apparent intention of going into exile in America. At Rochefort, however, he found the harbour blockaded and he decided to surrender himself to the Royal Navy. He was escorted aboard *HMS Bellerophon*. It was a new experience for him to see the inside of a ship of the Royal Navy, the instrument of France's defeat at Trafalgar a few years earlier. An English eyewitness on board noticed that 'he is extremely curious, and never passes anything remarkable in the ship without immediately demanding its use, and inquiring minutely into the manner thereof'.

'The important thing is not to stop questioning', said Einstein. 'Curiosity has its own reason for existing. One cannot help but be in awe when one contemplates the mysteries of eternity, of life, of the marvellous structure of reality. It is enough if one tries merely to comprehend a little of this mystery every day. Never lose a holy curiosity.'

Such curiosity is – or should be – the appetite of the intellect. Creative thinkers have it, because they need to be taking in information from many different sources. The novelist, William Trevor, for example, sees his role as an observer of human nature: 'You've got to like human beings, and be very curious,' he says, otherwise he doesn't think it is possible to write fiction.

Of course, curiosity in this sense must be distinguished from the sort of curiosity that proverbially kills the cat. The latter implies prying into other people's minds in an objectionable or intrusive way, or meddling in their personal affairs. True curiosity is simply the eager desire to learn and know. Such disinterested intellectual curiosity can become habitual. Leonardo da Vinci's motto was 'I question'.

'To be an inventor is an eclectic sort of life', said Sir Clive Sinclair. 'You've got to know about a lot of different subjects in different ways, so you have to teach yourself what you want to know. I don't think university is much of a help if you want to be an inventor – and that's all I ever wanted.'

One of the prime aims of education, it could be argued, is to develop such an inquisitive mind. 'The whole art of teaching,' wrote Anatole France, 'is only the art of awakening the natural curiosity of young minds for the purpose of satisfying it afterwards.'

'Curiouser and curiouser!' cried Alice in Wonderland. Too often it is only something curious, rare or strange that arouses our curiosity. But what excites attention merely because it is strange or odd is often not worth any further investigation. We do have to be selective in our curiosity.

There is a story about a young officer of whom it was said: 'His men will follow him anywhere – out of a sense of curiosity.' In creative thinking curiosity about what will happen next is an important ingredient in motivation. Ken Rowat makes that point:

> Creative activity, agonizing though it may be at times, is essentially life enhancing, often joyful, and this can be judged not from the fixed smiles worn by models advertising power tools but by the extent to which the individual is seriously engrossed in his activity. Outside making love, men and women never feel better than when they are totally engaged in exploration or construction, especially when the motivation is simply: 'I wonder what will happen if I do this?'

In other words, it is not simply a case of being curious in order to gather information, the raw materials of creative thought. Rather, creative thinking is itself a way of learning something new. You are not quite sure where your train of thought will lead you. So there is a connection between thinking and learning or rather trying to teach oneself.

'Thinking is trying to make up the gap in one's education', wrote the philosopher, Gilbert Ryle, in *On Thinking* (1979). It is not, of course, a matter of teaching yourself something that you want to know; you cannot teach it because you do not know it. 'What am I trying to think out for myself is indeed something that the Angel Gabriel conceivably might have known and taught me instead,' continued Ryle, 'but it is something that no one in fact did teach me. That is why I have to think. I swim because I am not a passenger on someone else's ferryboat. I think, as I swim, for myself. No one else could do this for me.'

KEYPOINTS

▓ 'Curiosity in children is but an appetite for knowledge', wrote the philosopher John Locke. You should aim to retain throughout your life that eager desire to see, learn or know. Curiosity is the mind on tiptoe.

▓ Creative thinkers tend to have a habit of curiosity that leads them to give searching attention to what interests them.

▓ Thinking is a way of trying to find out for yourself. If you always blindly accepted what others told you there would be nothing to be curious about.

▓ One way to develop your curiosity is to begin to ask more questions, both when you are talking with others and when you are talking in your mind to yourself. Questioning, carefully done, helps you to distinguish between what is known and what is unknown.

Go round asking a lot of damfool questions and taking chances. Only through curiosity can we discover opportunities, and only by gambling can we take advantage of them.
Clarence Birdseye, American industrialist

8

Keep your eyes open

Here is a great observer, and looks
Quite through the deeds of men.

William Shakespeare

If a man looks sharply and attentively, he shall see Fortune;
for though she is blind yet she is not invisible.

Francis Bacon

'I am fascinated by the principle of growth: how people and things evolved', said the portrait painter Graham Sutherland in an interview at the age of 73. He aimed to pin down the atmosphere and essence of the people he painted: 'I have to be as patient and watchful as a cat.' He could see in the human face the same sort of expression of the process of growth and struggle as he found in rugged surfaces of boulders or the irregular contours of a range of hills. 'There are so many ideas I want to get off my chest. The days aren't long enough', he added.

It may seem odd to think of painting a picture as a means of getting an idea off your chest. But for the artist the act of careful analytical observation is only part of the story. Ideas and emotions are fused into the paint in the heat of inspiration. What the artist knows and feels is married to what he or she sees, and the picture is the child of that union. 'Painting is a blind man's profession', said Picasso. 'He paints not what he sees, but what he feels, what he tells himself about what he has seen.' That principle holds true not only for the kind of art for which Picasso is famous but also for the more realistic work of painters such as Graham Sutherland.

An observation made through the eyes will undergo transformation to varying degrees in the creative mind as it is combined with other elements into a new idea, bubbling away in a cauldron of animated interest. As William Blake put it, 'A fool sees not the same tree that a wise man sees.' But the observation itself needs to be clear, accurate and honest. Like a good cook, a creative thinker should work from the best materials. Laurence Olivier was an actor renowned for his ability to build character in a creative way. 'I am like a scavenger,' he said, 'I observe closely, storing some details for as long as 18 years in my memory.' When invited to play the title role in Shakespeare's *King Richard the Third* he drew upon his recollection of Jed Harris, a famous Broadway producer of the 1930s under whom he had a bad experience. Harris had a prominent nose, which Olivier borrowed for the role, along with elements of his disagreeable character. But Olivier combined other elements into the new role, such as the shadow of the Big Bad Wolf, which he had seen long ago in

Walt Disney's film Pinocchio. Remembered films often gave him such ideas. The little dance he did while playing Shylock came from Hitler's jig for joy when France signed its capitulation in 1940, a moment shown on German newsreels.

Observation is a skill. 'You see, but you do not observe', comments Sherlock to his assistant Dr Watson in one of their cases. At the lowest level it implies the ability to see what is actually in front of you. As scientists know, this is not as easy as it sounds. It is almost impossible to be totally objective. We tend to see what we know already. That does leave some creative possibilities. For, as Gustave Flaubert wrote, 'There is an unexplored side to everything, because instead of looking at things with our eyes we look at them with the memory of what others have thought.'

Our minds are programmed to notice certain things rather than others, not least by our particular interests. A botanist, for instance, will be likely to notice plants. If we see things or people repeatedly we hardly observe them at all unless there is some change from the familiar or predictable, some deviation from the norm, which forces itself upon our attention. A good observer will be as objective as possible. Inevitably, he or she will be selective in observation, guided by some idea or principle on what to look for. But, being serendipitous, you should be sensitive to what you have not been told – or told yourself – to look for.

One of the best forms of training in observation is drawing or sketching. Take some paper and pencil and look at any object. Now select from what you see the key lines that give you its essential shape. You are now exercising careful analytical attention.

One of the great pioneers in the importance of teaching drawing was John Ruskin. As he told his students at the

Working Men's College in the 1850s, 'I am only trying to teach you to see.' Seeing, for Ruskin, was the fundamental way in which to acquire knowledge of the world, and it was a talent that few possessed. As he wrote in *Modern Painters*:

> the greatest thing a human soul ever does in this world is to *see* something, and tell what it *saw* in a plain way. Hundreds of people can talk for one who can think, but thousands can think for one who can see. To see clearly is poetry, prophecy and religion – all in one.

Do not worry if you cannot reproduce the object like a trained artist. Your aim is different. You are using sketching as a means of learning to use your eyes, so that you can really see the world around you. Such sketches, however rough and ready, will not only increase your awareness of the world but they will also help you to etch the scene in memory. In his autobiography, *A Millstone Round My Neck* (1983), the artist Norman Thelwell makes just that point:

> It may be that one's awareness of the world is heightened during the process of recording visual things with pencil, pen or brush. Sketchbooks and paintings, even the slightest notes, can recall not just the day and place but the hour, the moment, the sounds and smells that would have gone forever without them. I have drawings still which I did as a child and I can remember when I come across them what my brother said to me, what my mother was doing at the time, what was on the radio when I was working and how I felt about the world that day.

About 70 per cent of the information we use comes through our eyes. Therefore you should develop your ability to see things and make detailed observations. For they are the materials for future creative thinking.

KEYPOINTS

- The ability to give careful, analytical and honest attention to what you see is essential. If you do not notice and observe you will not think.

- Observation implies attempting to see a person, object or scene as if you had never seen it before in your life. What really teaches us, it has been said, is not experience, but observation.

- The act of observation is not complete until you have recorded what you have seen, thereby helping to commit it to memory. Observation capitalizes inspiration.

- A bystander may sometimes perhaps see more of the game than he who plays it. Watch less, observe more.

- 'All our knowledge has its origins in our perceptions', wrote Leonardo da Vinci. Do you see things clearly and accurately?

- Interested and close attention is the mother of perception. Sir Isaac Newton once told a friend: 'If I ever made any valuable discoveries, it has been owing more to patient attention than to any other talent.'

A good spectator also creates.

Swiss proverb

9

Listen for ideas

Give us grace to listen well.

John Keble

'You hear not what I say to you', said the Lord Chief Justice to Shakespeare's Falstaff. 'Very well, my Lord, very well', replies the irrepressible old rogue. 'Rather, if you will excuse me, it is the disease of not listening, the malady of not marking, that I am troubled with.'

Poor listening ability is a common affliction, but creative thinkers do not suffer from it. Although we know very little about Falstaff's creator we can at least surmise with some confidence that he was a good listener.

What constitutes such a rare beast as a good listener? First, a good listener will have curiosity, that all-essential desire to learn. That requires a degree of humility, the key to having an open mind. For if you think you know it all, or at least if you believe you know more than the person to whom you are talking, you are hardly inclined to listen. Hitler was an appallingly bad listener for that very reason.

Having an open mind does not guarantee that you will buy the idea, proposition or course of action being put to you. But it does mean that you are genuinely in the marketplace for new ideas. You will buy if the price is right. The next requirement is to control your analytical and critical urges. For your first priority is to grasp fully what the other person is actually saying, especially if it is a new and therefore strange idea to you. Have you a clear picture of it in your mind? A hearer only hears what the other person is saying; a listener discovers the real import of their words.

The act of comprehension, then, should come before the process of analysis and evaluation. Until you are clear about what is being said or suggested you are in no position to agree or accept.

A good listener is creative in the sense that he or she draws the best out of you. All professional musicians will tell you that the audience plays a vital part in a performance. Referring to a play that had recently failed, Oscar Wilde said: 'The play was a great success, but the audience was a disaster.'

One of the most creative listeners I have come across was Lord Roy Thomson of Fleet. In his autobiography, *Long After Sixty*, he had this to say about his policy of being a listener:

In my office I have always made myself accessible; I have always insisted upon this, to the extent often of not allowing my staff, or of not waiting for them, to vet strangers who came to see me before permitting them to come into my office. It is surprising the things that have sprung from this, the surprising things I've learned.

I am always curious, always hopeful. I still often duck out of an office meeting to see what some visitor looks like and to find out what he wants. Likewise, I take quite a few telephone calls if my secretary happens to be busy or out of the room for the moment; I have told the switchboard that if there is not one of my personal staff to answer a call, to put it straight through to me. I don't want any information or opportunity to go elsewhere just because no one could take a call.

I try to make friends wherever I go and it is my fond belief that I usually succeed. The way I look at it, everyone has an idea and one in a dozen may be a good idea. If you have to talk to a dozen people to get one good idea, that isn't wasteful work. People are continually passing things on to me, because I have given them to believe that I will be interested, I might even pay for it! Sometimes, usually when it is least expected, something comes up that is touched with gold.

Roy Thomson was full of questions on every subject. His interest was like a perennial spring: it flowed from the hope that the companion of the moment might add information to some current concern, or even reveal some world that Roy had not so far entered. He personified the Turkish proverb: 'Listening requires more intelligence than speaking.'

That may, however, be overstating the case. The ability to talk well and the ability to listen are, in fact, clearly related. As

Peter Ustinov once said to me, 'There is no point in talking without listening.' A person who listens because he or she has nothing to say can hardly be source of inspiration. The only listening that counts is that of the talker who alternately absorbs and expresses ideas.

KEYPOINTS

▪ A childlike curiosity and an open mind, backed up by sharp analytical skills and a sensitive judgement, are the essential prerequisites for being a good listener.

▪ Your priority must always be to achieve a grasp of the nature and significance of what is being said to you. Ask questions to elicit the full meaning. Understanding comes before evaluation.

▪ Listen for ideas, however incomplete and ambiguous, as well as for potentially relevant facts and information. 'My greatest strength as a consultant,' Peter Drucker once told me, 'is to be ignorant and ask a few questions.'

▪ Never miss a chance to shut up.

▪ The word *listen* contains the same letters as the word *silent*.

▪ 'It is the province of knowledge to speak, and it is the province of wisdom to listen', said Oliver Wendell Holmes.

Give every man your ear, but few your voice.
William Shakespeare

10

Reading to generate ideas

The use of reading is to aid us in thinking.
Edward Gibbon

'I love to lose myself in other men's minds', wrote Charles Lamb. 'When I am not walking, I am reading; I cannot sit and think. Books think for me.'

For many people, reading and research is more a device for avoiding thought rather than as an aid to it. But reading for diversion or entertainment, or reading merely for information, is different from reading for idea generation. What kinds of reading will develop your creative imagination?

Good fiction may come high on your list. Novelist John Fowles said that the reader of fiction has to take part and do half the work. 'I like the vagueness of the printed word', he said. Take a sentence like 'She walked across the road.' You have to imagine it, so you have freedom. No two people have ever imagined Tolstoy's characters in *War and Peace* in the same way. It makes for richness in reading, for it involves a communion between author and reader. Therefore prose and poetry will never die.

The words of Francis Clifford, writer of 15 novels, apply to all books likely to be useful to a creative thinker. 'A writer's task', he said, 'is not to spell everything out. It is really to imply and infer and hint, to give the reader the opportunity of total involvement by encouraging him or her to contribute his or her own reflections and imagery.'

Reading without reflecting has been compared to eating without digesting. 'Some books are to be tasted, others to be swallowed, and some few to be chewed and digested', Francis Bacon put it more accurately. One page or even one paragraph properly digested will be more fruitful than a whole volume hurriedly read. Or, as the film mogul, Sam Goldwyn, said to a hopeful author, 'I have read part of your book all the way though.' When you come across significant parts – the passages that speak to you – it is worth remembering the counsel of the *Book of Common Prayer*: 'Read, mark, learn, and inwardly digest.'

No good book, any more than helpful words, can do anything decisive if the person concerned is not already prepared through quite invisible influences for a deeper receptivity and absorption. For the only books that really influence us are those for which we are ready, and which have gone a little further down our particular path than we have yet gone ourselves.

The power of a good book is in the intimate relationship of author and reader. It is a transaction that takes place in solitude. It invites you to think for yourself about some subject away from the context of other people. The author should be able to lead you to nourishing food or refreshing water, and, though he or she cannot make you drink, he or she should provide you with plenty of encouragement to do so. These almost unique conditions of inner dialogue enable a good book to reach deep into your consciousness.

You don't have to plod through a book from page one to the end. You can skip and skim. Therefore there is little point in taking a speed reading course. 'I am not a speed reader,' said space fiction writer Isaac Asimov, 'I am a speed understander.' Taste the contents, then select what you wish to chew and swallow. Never swallow first, for if you believe everything you read it is better not to read.

The delights of reading in this spirit are legendary. We can travel in time, transcending our own culture and our own day. For, as Descartes wrote, 'To converse with those of other centuries is almost the same as travelling.' Remember the points in earlier chapters: you may discover ideas, practices, facts or technologies in these distant times and places that suddenly connect with your present interests and concerns. You may be surprised to discover the unexpected by happy serendipity.

Did you know, for example, that:

- Solomon's temple was protected by lightning rods?

- Nero devised a coin-in-the-slot machine?

- The Caesars had three elevators in their palace?

- Hindus used the cowpox virus centuries before Jenner?

- The reaping machine was described as a 'worn-out French invention' in the 16th century?

- A thousand years before Christ, the Chinese extracted digitalis from living toads to treat heart disease, recorded earthquakes undetected by the human senses, and used an instrument that always pointed north?

Reading books, then, can stimulate and develop your powers of creative thinking. If nothing else, a good book can put you into a working mood. If you are resolved to devote as much time and attention on your mental fitness as a thinker as the average person spends on that more wasting asset, the human body, you will be inclined to follow Charles Darwin's advice:

> If I had my life to live over again, I would have made a rule to read some poetry and listen to some music at least once a week; for perhaps the parts of my brain now atrophied would thus have been kept active through use. The loss of these tastes is a loss of happiness, and may possibly be injurious to the intellect, and more probably to the moral character, by enfeebling the emotional part of our nature.

Darwin, incidentally, was a remarkably accomplished painter as well as being an extraordinary scientist.

KEYPOINTS

■ Nothing is worth reading that does not require an alert mind, open and eager to learn.

■ Books are storehouses of ideas, thoughts, facts, opinions, descriptions, information and dreams. Some of these, removed from their setting, may connect to your present (or future) interests as a thinker.

■ 'Reading is to the mind what exercise is to the body', wrote Sir Richard Steele. Poetry and good prose – fact or fiction – requires the use of your imaginative and recreative powers. Therefore they provide you with an enjoyable way of developing those faculties.

■ The real object of education is to take you to the condition of continuously asking questions.

■ Under the hospitable roof of *reading, studying* and *learning* you will also find housed *inspiring, kindling* and *infecting*.

■ 'Reading furnishes the mind only with materials of knowledge; it is thinking that makes what we read ours', wrote John Locke.

Learning is like rowing upstream; not to advance is to drop back.

Chinese proverb

11

Keep a notebook

A commonplace book contains many notions in garrison, whence the owner may draw out an army into the field on competent warning.

Thomas Fuller

'The horror of that moment,' the King went on, 'I shall never, *never* forget!' 'You will, though,' the Queen said, 'If you don't make a memorandum of it.' This advice from Lewis Carroll in *Alice in Wonderland* certainly applies in the field of creative thinking. One practical step you can take now is to buy a new notebook to record possible materials for your present or future use: ideas, a scrap of conversation, something seen or heard on television or radio, a quotation from an article or book, an observation, a proverb. Write it down!

You have probably had the experience of waking up in the middle of the night with an idea. It was such a good one that you told yourself to remember it next morning. But, like the memory of your dreams, it fades fast away. 'Every composer knows,' Hector Berlioz said, 'the anguish and despair occasioned by forgetting ideas which one has not had time to write down.' He spoke from experience, he added. Keep a pencil and pad by your bed. Carry a pocket notebook so that ideas that strike you while waiting for someone or travelling on a train can be recorded. Later you can transfer these jottings to your main notebook.

Apart from reinforcing and extending memory, the practice of keeping a commonplace book of notable passages or quotations in particular has one fairly obvious further benefit. The labour of copying them out gives you occasion to reflect deeply on them. For, as you slowly write or type, you have to pay attention to both the exact form and the content of what is being said. The act of writing impresses the words more deeply on your mind. Once a thought is in your own handwriting you have appropriated it personally: it is now numbered among the ideas and influences that matter to you.

There are two important principles in keeping a commonplace notebook as a tool for creative thinking. First, put down entries in the order in which they occur to you. Give a short title to the entry, and perhaps a date. Do not try to be too systematic, by putting everything on cards or loose-leaf paper arranged alphabetically, indexed and cross-indexed. If you are a scientist, for example, that may be the right method. But that is not the best way when it comes to developing your powers as a creative thinker.

The second principle is to let your instinct or intuitive sense decide what you think is worth noting down. Include whatever impresses you as stimulating, interesting or memorable.

At this stage it doesn't matter too much if the idea is right or wrong, only that it is interesting. Later – months later – you may need to do some editing, but initially what matters is whether or not the prospective entry gives you a spontaneous reaction of excitement or deep interest. As Shakespeare wrote: 'No profit grows where is no pleasure taken.'

In this form your commonplace notebook is a very useful tool for creative thinking on a variety of subjects that concern you. For this method brings together very diverse material. When you look through your notebook you will begin to notice various constellations of links and connections. It is this coming together of elements hitherto unrelated – the interaction of unlikely bedfellows – that makes a notebook of this nature a veritable seedbed of new ideas.

Here are some practical suggestions. Use hardcover books, but not large or bulky ones. Ledgers are too heavy to carry around. Leave a large margin and plenty of space above and below, so that you can add some notes in pencil later. You may like to write in different coloured inks. The margin can also be used for cross-referencing. Number the pages and then you can add a simple index at the back by subject.

Do not look at your entries too often. In my experience, the best time to browse though them creatively (unless, that is, you are hunting for a reference for a specific purpose) is on a train or air journey, waiting in airports, or on holiday when the mind is fresh and unencumbered with daily business.

KEYPOINTS

▨ Keeping a notebook is more than a useful habit: it is a vitally important tool for all creative thinking purposes.

▨ 'A man would do well to carry a pencil in his pocket,' said Francis Bacon, 'and write down the thoughts of the moment. Those that come unsought are commonly the most valuable and should be secured, because they seldom return.'

▨ Writing down a quotation or passage, fact or piece of information, is a means of meditating upon it and appropriating it personally so that it grows into part of you.

▨ Imagine that your notebook is like a kaleidoscope. At a time when you are feeling in a creative frame of mind, give it a metaphorical shake. You can play with new combinations and interconnections. They may suggest new ideas or lines of thought.

▨ Don't forget to add inspirational quotations, stories and examples to your own personal collection. For creative thinking calls for stimulus, encouragement and inspiration. If you build a positive orientation of mind you will become increasingly more creative in your thinking.

Many ideas grow better when transplanted into another mind than in the one where they sprung up.
Oliver Wendell Holmes

12

Test your assumptions

If a man begins with certainties he shall end in doubts;
but if he will be content to begin with doubts he will end
with certainties.

Francis Bacon

Einstein is famous for making one assumption and thinking out its implications. 'Let me assume,' he said to himself, 'that I am riding on the back of a sunbeam, travelling though the universe with the speed of light. How would things look to me?' The eventual result was the General Theory of Relativity. By it Einstein led us to the knowledge that planets and stars move not because they are influenced by forces coming from other bodies in the universe, but because of the special nature of the world of space and time in the neighbourhood of matter. Light-rays may travel straight, for example, in the vast interstellar spaces, but they are deflected or bent when they come within the field of influence of a star or other massive body.

Making *conscious* assumptions like that one is a key tool in the tool chest of a creative thinker. You are *deliberately* and *temporarily* making a supposition that something is true. It is like making a move in a game of chess but still keeping your hand on the piece, so that you can replace it if you do not like the implications of the half-made move. 'No great discovery is made without a bold guess', said Isaac Newton.

I have emphasized the words above in italics because this kind of exploratory thinking does need to be sharply distinguished from thinking based upon unconscious assumptions or preconceptions. We have all had the experience of taking something for granted as the basis for opinion or action, and then subsequently finding that we had made an assumption – probably an unconscious one – that was unwarranted.

Watch out for these preconceptions! They are like hidden sandbanks outside the harbour mouth. Preconceived ideas are the ones you entertain before actual knowledge. The really dangerous ones are those below your level of awareness.

For we take on board all sorts of assumptions and preconceptions, often in the form of opinions or commonsense, which on examination turn out to be unproven or debatable. They are the main impediments to having new ideas. Take a look at the exercise below:

EXERCISE

On a spare piece of paper draw a square of nine dots like this:

Now see if you can connect up the dots with four consecutive straight lines, that is, without taking your pencil off the paper. You have one minute to complete the task.

For the answer, see page 127 in Appendix C at the back of the book.

Received opinion on anything should be suspect. Once an idea is generally accepted it is time to consider rejecting it. But it is very difficult for you to do that. For, to borrow Einstein's language, people in the mass can influence the space around them, deflecting the pure shaft of human thought.

'Few people,' said Einstein, 'are capable of expressing with equanimity opinions which differ from the prejudices of their social environment. Most people are even incapable of forming such opinions.' We are social thinkers. Often great thinkers are rather solitary figures, possibly because they have a need to distance themselves psychologically from the powerful influences of received opinion.

When it comes to those dangerous unconscious assumptions, other people can be especially helpful to you. They can sometimes alert you to the fact that you are *assuming* that something is the case without being aware that you are doing so. 'Why do you believe that?' they ask. 'What is your evidence? Who told you that you could not?'

Assumptive thinking is not the same as guessing. When we conjecture, surmise or guess we are really drawing inferences from slight evidence. Guessing means hitting upon a conclusion either wholly at random or from very uncertain evidence. Making an assumption is more like taking a tentative step. '*Supposing* we did it this way – how would it work? What would the consequences be?' It is not an answer – even a guessed answer – but it is a step that you can take if you are baffled, which might open up new possibilities.

It is more important to appreciate this difference between deliberately preconceived ideas and fixed ideas, often unconsciously held. 'Preconceived ideas are like searchlights which illumine the path of an experimenter and serve him as a guide to interrogate nature', said Louis Pasteur. 'They become a danger only if he transforms them into fixed ideas – that is why I should like to see these profound words inscribed on the threshold of all the temples of science: "The greatest derangement of the mind is to believe in something because one wishes it to be so." '

Getting the balance right between imaginative thinking and critical thinking is essential for all creative thinkers, not least research scientists. Pasteur continued: 'Imagination is needed to give wings to thought at the beginning of experimental investigation into any given subject. When, however, the time has come to conclude, and to interpret the facts derived from observation, imagination must submit to the factual results of the experiments.'

Consequently, thinking will lead you to break or bend some of the rules that others take to be axiomatic. It is a fairly well-established rule in thinking that you should not base an argument on false premises. For the purposes of creative thinking, however, 'a false premise' in the shape of a bold and imaginative assumption may be just what you need in order to shatter your preconception. 'Daring ideas are like chessmen moved forward', writes Goethe. 'They may be beaten, but they may start a winning game.'

KEYPOINTS

▪ The ability to explore possible ways forward by making some deliberate assumptions is important. They are to be made without commitment, like trying on new clothes in a shop before buying (or not buying) them.

▪ Develop your awareness of the jungle of tangled misconceptions, preconceptions and unconscious assumptions within you. Welcome others when they challenge or test your assumptions.

▪ Opinions are often more precious than true. They change according to such factors as the group organization or society, time and place where you happen to be.

▪ Today's commonsense is very different from commonsense 50 years ago. What will commonsense be like, what kinds of opinion will there be, in 50 years' time?

▪ Think outside the box! Don't allow yourself to be constrained by the mental limitations or straitjackets that are sometimes imposed on situations without any warrant or truth.

Imagination is the vision that sees the possibilities of the materials and resources we have.

Anon

13

Make better use of your Depth Mind

While the fisher sleeps the net takes the fish.
Ancient Greek Proverb

The fact that the unconscious mind plays a part in decision-making, problem-solving and creative thinking has been known for some time. This dimension I have named 'the Depth Mind', and it is arguably the most important element in creative thinking.

In my previous books I have quoted a number of examples of the Depth Mind at work, and I have dozens more in my files. Doubtless you can add to the list as well. The big question is whether or not we can learn how to make better use of our Depth Mind in order to generate new ideas.

First, however, let us clear out of the way the question of the location of creative thinking in the brain, for it is relatively unimportant. Relatively recent discoveries of the brain suggest that there may be two different kinds of intelligence – analytic, conceptual, verbal intelligence, located in the left hemisphere of the brain, and intuitive, artistic intelligence in the right hemisphere. Hence a spate of books on 'Right Brain' thinking.

Now this research is a good example of the tendency to dichotomize things being projected onto the evidence. Dividing things sharply into two camps, like black and white, is a good teaching device, but it almost invariably leads to over-simplification of what is in fact very complex. For in creative thinking, for example, analytical and critical faculties of the mind come into play as well as the synthesizing faculty. Both sides of the brain are involved.

A FRAMEWORK OF EFFECTIVE THINKING

I suggest that when we are thinking, three basic functions are either at work or waiting their turn to come into play:

- *Analysing*. The taking to pieces; resolving an entity into its constituent elements. The original meaning was literally 'to dissect'. The application to abstract objects emerged from the 18th century.

■ *Synthesizing.* From the Greek verb 'to set free, to loosen'. The building up of a complex whole by the union of elements, especially the process of forming concepts, general ideas, theories, etc.

■ *Valuing.* The assessing of worth or value, especially as compared with other things. From the Latin verb valere, 'to be strong', 'to be worth'.

You will notice that the first two mental functions are related. *Analysing* is separating a whole into its component parts. *Synthesizing* is the reverse process of building up elements into a complex or coherent whole. *Valuing,* however, comes from a different family. Our capacity to value is innate, but our actual valuing (or 'values') is conditioned by our particular cultural situation in life. How far it is true that there are universal 'values' – good, truth and beauty for example – is a philosophical question that lies beyond the scope of this book. In my view, for what it is worth, there are. Our valuing faculty, I believe, is rather like a radar that is capable of identifying real values 'out there' when they appear on its inner screen. Our ability to recognize the truth of propositions, such as $2 + 2 = 4$, strikes me as an obvious example.

Valuing is related to creative thinking because the very concept of creative is a value-laden one. Hence we reserve the word for only certain kinds of new wholes, as contrasted to the sea of novelties that crowd in upon us. To call something creative implies that it has real extrinsic or intrinsic value.

EMOTION

Psychologists (who tend to be analysts by disposition) tend to divide the human mind into *cognitive* – knowing, perceiving or conceiving – and *affective* – feeling, emotion or desire – and *volitional* – the exercise of will. But in practice, thinking and feeling and willing are almost indistinguishable, for we only have one mind housed in one brain.

Emotion and *motive* stem from the same Latin verb 'to move'. I compare emotion to the electricity that makes a computer work. As we all know, too much emotion – especially the negative emotions of fear, anxiety or panic – can cloud thinking to the extent that it is virtually impossible to think clearly or creatively. On the other hand, a positive, mental climate – warm interest, curiosity, confidence – can foster the optimum use of your mind's resources. An effective thinker is always a wise manager of his or her emotions.

Certainly, creative people tend to have a strong emotional investment in their work. The great engineer, Isambard Kingdom Brunel, wrote about the Clifton suspension bridge in his diary as if it were a beloved person: 'My child, my darling is actually going on – recommenced last week – Glorious!'

DEPTH MIND

I use the metaphor of the submarine at sea to illustrate that thinking can sometimes leave the surface and proceed on its voyage many fathoms below in the depth of the sea. Then it can surface again into the conscious mind.

Far from being merely chaotic, a repository of suppressed memories and emotions as some of the Freudians taught, the unconscious mind is capable of purposeful work. What is going on down there? The short answer is that nobody knows.

My own theory, one that has stood the test of time, is that the Depth Mind has its own capability for analysing, synthesizing and valuing. And when it has done its work it sometimes – not unlike a computer – prints out its findings or solutions into our consciousness. Of course these 'printouts' are not always ideas that are imaginative or creative in the sense of being new and valuable 'wholes' presenting themselves gift-wrapped to the mind.

Most of us have experienced such products of the Depth Mind as *intuitions* – immediate perceptions of the mind without reasoning – *hunches*, *premonitions* and *inklings*. For creative thinkers, inklings – an intimation of something yet unknown – are especially important, for they may be signals that one is on the right track. It doesn't require prophetic powers or extra-sensory perception. What happens is that your Depth Mind is at work, interpreting natural signs, picking up hints that invade your senses below the conscious threshold, and piecing together the paucity of information in the shape of guesses, hints or clues. Sometimes, for example, there may be a feeling of pleasure or excitement that precedes discovery but again indicates that one is groping in the right direction.

To understand the workings of the Depth Mind – at least for me to convince you that I am not making it up! – let's look at some case studies of what outstanding artists say about the business of creation – *the entire process whereby things that did not exist before are conceived, given form and brought into being.*

The case of the great composers

Tchaikovsky wrote this description of his Depth Mind at work:

> Sometimes I observe with curiosity that uninterrupted activity, which – independent of the subject of any conversation I may be carrying on – continues its course in that department of my brain which is devoted to music. Sometimes it takes a preparatory form – that is, the consideration of all details that concern the elaboration of some projected work; another time it may be an entirely new and independent musical idea.

The case of C S Forester, author of the *Hornblower* books

The creative process is much more like a seed being implanted and fusing with another already present, which then grows by a form of accretion. In his autobiography *Long Before Forty* (1967), the novelist had written one of the best introspective descriptions of what he sensed was going on in his Depth Mind.

Notice his imaginative use of analogy (see Chapter 3) to take us forward in understanding:

> There are jellyfish that drift about in the ocean. They do nothing to seek out their daily food; chance carries them hither and thither, and chance brings them nourishment. Small living things come into contact with their tentacles, and are seized, devoured and digested. Think of me as the jellyfish, and the captured victims become the plots, the

stories, the outlines, the motifs – use whatever term you may consider best to describe the framework of a novel. In the ocean there are much higher forms of life than jellyfish, and every human being in the ocean of humanity has much the same experience as every other human being, but some human beings are jellyfish and some are sharks. The tiny little food particles, the minute suggestive experiences, are recognized and seized by the jellyfish writer and are employed by him for his own specialized use.

We can go on with the analogy; once the captured victim is inside the jellyfish's stomach the digestive juices start pouring out and the material is transformed into a different protoplasm, without the jellyfish consciously doing anything about it until his existence ends with an abrupt change of analogy.

In my own case it happens that, generally speaking, the initial stimulus is recognized for what it is. The casual phrase dropped by a friend in conversation, the paragraph in a book, the incident observed by the roadside, has some special quality, and is accorded a special welcome. But having been welcomed, it is forgotten or at least ignored. It sinks into the horrid depths of my subconscious like a water-logged timber into the slime at the bottom of a harbour, where it lies alongside others which have preceded it. Then, periodically – but by no means systematically – it is hauled up for examination along with its fellows, and sooner or later, some timber is found with barnacles growing on it. Some morning when I am shaving, some evening when I am wondering whether my dinner calls for white wine or red, the original immature idea reappears in my mind, and it has grown. Nearly always it has something to do with what eventually will be the mid-point of a novel or a short story, and sometimes the growth is towards the end and sometimes towards the beginning. The casualty rate is high – some timbers grow no barnacles at all – but enough of them have progressed to keep me actively employed for more than forty years.

Perhaps the best commentary on C S Forester's classic picture of the Depth Mind at work comes from the pen of another eminent writer, E M Forster: 'In the creative state,' he writes, 'a man is taken out of himself. He lets down as it were a bucket into his subconscious, and draws up something which is normally beyond his reach. He mixes this thing with his normal experience, and out of the mixture he makes a work of art.'

Obviously some vocations – authors, inventors, playwrights, scientists and composers for example – call more for such Depth Mind activity than others. But the ability to make such connections, to grow new ideas or wholes, is present in all of us in varying degrees. The first step is to understand that your mind does have a Depth Mind dimension. With a degree of simple awareness, understanding and skill you can work with its holistic capability of growing ideas as if they were seeds connecting or integrating apparently unrelated materials, creating order out of chaos. Skill? Yes, because there is an art in knowing when to stand back and let your Depth Mind do its work.

KEYPOINTS

■ According to an old English proverb, 'There is a great deal of unmapped country within us.' In part, creative thinking is about exploring and fathering an unknown hinterland.

■ The functions of the conscious mind – analysing, synthesizing and valuing – can also take place at a deeper level. Your Depth Mind can dissect something for you, just as your stomach juices can break down food into its elements.

■ The Depth Mind, for example, is capable of analysing data that you may not have known you had taken in, and comparing it with what is filed away in your memory bank.

■ The Depth Mind is capable of more than analysis. It is also close to the seat of your memory and the repository of your values. It is also a workshop where creative syntheses can be made by an invisible workmanship.

■ We can, of course, all synthesize consciously. We can put two and two together to make four, or we can assemble bits of leather together to make a shoe. But creative synthesis is likely to be characterized by the combination of unlikely elements, distant from or apparently (to others) unrelated to one another. And/or the raw materials used will have undergone a significant transformation. When this kind of synthesis is required, the Depth Mind comes into its own.

■ An organic analogy for its function is the womb, where after conception a baby is formed and grown from living matter. The word holistic, which applies to nature's tendency to grow wholes from seeds, aptly applies to the synthesizing processes of the inner brain in the realm of ideas. A baby is always a whole. Hence a new idea, concept or project is sometimes called a 'brain-child'.

▪ You may also have experienced the value thinking of the Depth Mind's neighbour we call conscience in the form of guilt feelings or even remorse when it has made a moral evaluation or judgement of your own conduct. This unwanted and unasked contribution to your sanity is a reminder that the Depth Mind has a degree of autonomy from you. It is not your slave. Henry Thoreau once boldly suggested that 'the unconsciousness of man is the consciousness of God'.

There is a dark
Inscrutable workmanship that reconciles
Discordant elements, makes them cling together
In one society.

William Wordsworth

14

Do not wait for inspiration

Thou, O God, dost sell us all good things at the price of labour.

Leonardo da Vinci

'I can call spirits from the vastly deep', boasts Owen Glendower in Shakespeare's *Henry IV*. Hotspur puts down the fiery Celt by replying: 'Why so can I, or so can any man; but will they come when you do call for them?' Doubtless Shakespeare is writing here from personal experience. The comings and goings of inspiration are unpredictable.

In creative work it is unwise to wait for the right mood. Graham Greene once said:

> Writing has to develop its own routine. When I'm seriously at work on a book, I set to work first thing in the morning, about seven or eight o'clock, before my bath or shave, before I've looked at my post or done anything else. If one had to wait for what people call 'inspiration', one would never write a word.

The thriller writer Leslie Thomas agreed:

> People are always asking me, 'Do you wait for inspiration?' But any novelist who does that is going to starve. I sit down, usually without an idea in my head, and stare at the proverbial blank paper; once I get going, it just *goes.*

It can seem impossible, like trying to drive a car with more water in the tank than petrol. But you just have to get out and push. Better to advance by inches than not to advance at all.

Thomas Edison, inventor of the electric light bulb among many other things, gave a celebrated definition of genius as '1 per cent inspiration and 99 per cent perspiration'. Creative thinking, paradoxically, is for 99 hours out of every 100 not very creative: it is endlessly varied combinations of analysing, synthesizing, imagining and valuing. The raw materials are sifted, judged, adapted, altered and glued together in different ways. When Queen Victoria congratulated the world-renowned pianist Paderewski on being a genius he replied: 'That may be, Ma'am, but before I was a genius I was a drudge.'

Not all intellectual drudges, however, are geniuses. Something more is needed. That lies beyond the willingness to start work without tarrying for inspiration and to keep at it day in and day out. You also need a peculiar kind of sensitivity, as if you were standing still and waiting, prepared and ready with all your senses alert, for the faintest marching of the wind in the treetops. Your spiritual eye may trace some delicate motion in your deeper mind, some thought that stirs like a leaf in the unseen air. It is not the stillness, nor the breath making the embers glow, nor the half-thought that only stirred, but these three mysteries in one that together constitute the experience of inspiration.

The German poet Goethe used a more homely image:

> The worst is that the very hardest thinking will not bring thoughts. They must come like good children of God and cry 'Here we are'. But neither do they come unsought. You expend effort and energy thinking hard. Then, after you have given up, they come sauntering in with their hands in their pockets. If the effort had not been made to open the door, however, who knows if they would have come?

One incident in the life of James Watt illustrates Goethe's principle beautifully. Watt found that the condenser for the Newcomen steam engine, which he studied at the University of Glasgow, was very inefficient. Power for each stroke was developed by first filling the cylinder with steam and then cooling it with a jet of water. This cooling action condensed the steam and formed a vacuum behind the piston, which the pressure of the atmosphere then forced to move. Watt calculated that this process of alternately heating and cooling of the cylinder wasted three-quarters of the heat supplied to the engine. Therefore Watt realized that if he could prevent this loss he could reduce the engine's fuel consumption by more than 50 per cent. He worked for two years on the problem with no solution in sight. Then, one fine Sunday afternoon, he was out walking:

I had entered the green and had passed the old washing house. I was thinking of the engine at the time. I had gone as far as the herd's house when the idea came into my mind that as steam was an elastic body it would rush into a vacuum, and if a connection were made between the cylinder and an exhausting vessel it would rush into it and might then be condensed without cooling the cylinder ... I had not walked further than the Golf house when the whole thing was arranged in my mind.

'Like a long-legged fly upon the stream, her mind moves upon silence.' These evocative words of Robert Frost underline the need for silence and solitude in creative thinking, such as you find on a country walk. It helps, too, if you have a feeling of expectancy or confidence. We have all been given minds capable of creative thinking and there is no going back on that. So we are more than halfway there. We just have to believe that there are words and music in the air, so to speak, if we tune in our instruments to the right wavelengths. They will come in their own time and place. Our task is to be ready for them. For inspiration, like chance, favours the prepared mind. By contrast, negative feelings of fear, anxiety or worry, even anxiety that inspiration will never come or never return – are antithetical to this basic attitude of trust. They drive away what they long for. 'If winter comes, can spring be far behind?'

KEYPOINTS

■ The Depth Mind is a rendezvous. It is as if it is sometimes a meeting place between human thought and divine inspiration, issuing in genuinely creative ideas and new creations.

■ That, of course, is only an assumption or, if you prefer it, an unproven hypothesis. Whether true or not, it may be a useful and productive strategy to act as if it were true.

■ Creative thinkers of all kinds – including scientists – tend to retain a spiritual model of inspiration, if only in their awareness of an unfathomable and unanalysable mystery in how true creation or discovery occurs.

■ You and I may have and develop a talent for creative thinking, but others clearly have a gift, which is something of a different quality and degree. Who is the giver? How is the gift given? What is its nature? How is it best preserved? Can it be lost?

■ Do not wait for inspiration or you will wait for ever. Inspiration is a companion that will appear beside you on certain stretches of the road. 'One sits down first,' said Jean Cocteau, 'one thinks afterwards.'

■ 'The intellect has little to do on the road to discovery', said Einstein. 'There comes a leap in consciousness, call it intuition or what you will, and the solution comes to you and you don't know how or why.'

■ Develop an inner sensitivity or awareness, so that your spiritual eyes and ears are open to the slightest movement or suggestion from outside or inside, from above or below, which hints at a way forward. Listen to your inklings!

▪ You cannot quite control the process that leads to genuine creative work. But having the right attitude of expectancy, together with a measure of hope and confidence, certainly seems to pay off.

> *It is no good trying to shine if you don't take time to fill your lamp.*
>
> *Robert Frost*

15

Sharpen your analytical skills

One should never impose one's views on a problem; one should rather study it, and in time a solution will reveal itself.

Albert Einstein

'Often I feel frustrated when I am thinking about something', said the scientist and banker, Lord Rothschild, a Fellow of the Royal Society and first director of the British Government's 'Think Tank'. He was, he said, a good analyst but not a truly creative thinker. 'Synthetic thinking, creative thinking if you like, is a higher order altogether. People who think creatively hear the music of the spheres. I have heard them once or twice.'

Now Rothschild is obviously correct in believing that we all have different profiles of strengths and weaknesses as thinkers. Creative thinkers are clearly stronger in synthesizing and in their imagination. But the best of them are equally strong in their analysing ability and the faculty of valuing or judging. It is this combination of mental strengths, supported by some important personal qualities or characteristics that make for a formidable creative mind.

All these abilities – analysing, synthesizing and valuing – are at work when you are attempting to think creatively. In some phases or passages of the mind's work one will be more dominant than the other two, but they are never wholly absent. That is partly why creative thinking cannot be broken down into a process (as psychological analysts have constantly attempted to do), still less a system. It is not a stately procession from analysis to synthesis, and from synthesis to evaluation.

The nearest approach to identifying an underlying process is the one made by Graham Wallas in *The Art of Thought* (1926). He proposed that the germination of original ideas passes through four phases:

1. preparation;

2. incubation;

3. illumination; and

4. verification.

Now this is over-simplified, for creative thinkers may not follow that sequence, but it is nonetheless a useful framework.

The first characteristic of original thinking, according to Wallas, in a wide spectrum of fields, is a period of intense application, of immersion in a particular problem, question or issue. It is followed by a period when conscious attention is switched away from the topic, either by accident or design (the incubation phase). Sometimes there follows a sudden flash of insight or intuition (illumination) followed by a period when the idea is subjected to critical tests and then modified (the verification stage).

My own perspective is slightly different. There is a conscious phase when you are aware of predominantly trying to analyse the matter that has engaged your attention. You may play around with some restructuring of it (synthesizing). Some valuing will enter into it – 'Is it worthwhile spending time on this project?' Your imagination may also get to work, picturing some of the obvious solutions that occur to you or their consequences. You may also be giving yourself advice or asking yourself questions, such as 'Remember not to accept the first solution that comes to mind' or 'Am I making any unconscious assumptions?' This phase corresponds to Wallas's 'preparation', but that label is misleading because we may revert quite often to this conscious working of our minds.

When we are not so engaged, these activities of analysing, synthesizing and valuing can continue – but they do not do so invariably – at the level of our Depth or 'unconscious' Minds. We may then receive the products of such subliminal thinking in a variety of ways. The American poet Amy Lowell, for instance, said, 'I meet them where they touch consciousness, and that is already a considerable distance along the road to evolution.'

This reception of an idea from the unconscious mind to the consciousness is far from being the end of the story; it is only a halfway stage. During the process of working out, other fresh ideas and developments of a creative kind will still occur. Things are made in the making.

The object of analysis is clarity of thought. For clear thinking should precede and accompany creative thinking. What is the focus of your thinking? Is it some necessity, some everyday problem, or a resource that could be exploited in several different ways? If it is a problem, what are the success criteria for any satisfactory solution?

Check your definition of the problem (see Appendix A, page 119). Are you rating symptoms rather than the disease? There are often several equally valid (but not equally obvious) ways of defining any problem. But each definition is a general statement of a potential solution to the problem. So different definitions are worth collecting: they are signposts for different avenues of thought. The definition you settle upon may have a powerful influence in programming your Depth Mind. If it leads nowhere, try another definition.

Edward Jenner's discovery of vaccination illustrates how useful it is to be able to redefine the problem. At the end of the 18th century, Jenner took the first step towards ending the scourge of smallpox when he turned from the question of why people caught the disease to why dairymaids did not: the answer being that they were immunized by exposure to the relatively harmless cowpox.

Two men were walking in the African bush when they met a very hungry cheetah who eyed them ferociously. One of the men fished out some running shoes from his knapsack and bent down to put them on. 'Why are you doing that?' cried his companion in despair. 'Don't you know that cheetahs can run at over 60 miles per hour?' 'Yes, yes,' he replied as he finished tying his laces, 'but I only have to outrun you.'

The best advice is not to focus too strongly on any aspect of the problem. You should learn to think generally about it, like a scientist scanning a problem area for clues. Let it speak to you. 'Whatever the ultimate object of his work,' wrote Hazel Rossotti, in *Introducing Chemistry*, 'the experimental chemist's immediate aim is to ask suitable questions of the sensible bodies he is studying and to *let them answer for themselves*. It is the chemist's job to observe and report the answers with minimal distortion; only then can he attempt to interpret them.' These attitudes, a proper detachment and objectivity, are relevant to creative thinkers in the conscious phases of their work.

It is so easy to introduce subjective elements – such as those troublesome unconscious assumptions or constraints – into the problem or matter under review. Patient analysis and restructuring of the parts, taking up different perspective points in your imagination from which to view it: all these will deepen your understanding of the problem if they do not fairly soon release within you, like a cash dispenser, the right solution or at least the right direction in which to advance.

KEYPOINTS

▪ 'There is no expedient to which a man will not resort to avoid the real labour of thinking', said Sir Joshua Reynolds. Are you willing to devote some time and effort to the problems that face you? See them not as problems but opportunities to practise your skills as a thinker.

▪ The skill of analysing – taking things to bits in order to discern underlying principles or ideas – is a key implement in the tool chest of a creative thinker.

▪ There is no standard process or system of creative thinking; there is no system that you can learn. For creative thinking is essentially about freedom. To think freely means to be free from processes, systems and drills.

▪ The best creative minds are those that have been subjected to various disciplines when young, and then have reverted back to their natural proclivities.

▪ When analysing do not be over-hasty in defining the problem. Play with alternative formulations until one emerges that commands your support.

In a million people there are a thousand thinkers, in a thousand thinkers there is one self-thinker.

Anon

16

Suspend judgement

Criticism often takes from the tree caterpillars and blossoms together.

Jean-Paul Sartre

The German poet Johann Schiller wrote the following some 200 years ago:

> In the case of the creative mind, it seems to me it is as if the intellect has withdrawn its guards from the gates; ideas rush in pell mell and only then does it review and examine the multitude. You worthy critics, or whatever you may call yourselves, are ashamed or afraid of the momentary and passing madness found in all real creators... Hence your complaints of unfruitfulness – you reject too soon and discriminate too severely.

There are two important points here. First, we tend to post 'guards' on our minds. We criticize or evaluate our own ideas – or half ideas – far too soon. Criticism, especially the wholly negative kind, can be like a cold, white frost in spring: it kills off seeds and budding leaves. If we can relax our self-critical guard and let ideas come sauntering in, then we shall become more productive thinkers. Don't confuse evaluation with idea fluency. Be as prolific as you can with ideas until you find one that satisfies you. Then try to translate it into the form you want.

Second, beware of critics! Some people are just too critical. There is a Chinese saying to that effect: 'He could find fault with a bird on the wing'. Any sensible person should, of course, be open to the criticism of others. It is one of the offices of a friend, if no one else, to offer you constructive criticism about your work and perhaps also about your personal conduct. If we did not have this form of feedback we should never improve. But there is a time and place for everything. The time is not when you are exploring and experimenting with new ideas. This is the reason why professional creative thinkers – authors, inventors and artists, for example – seldom talk about work in progress.

Certain environments are notoriously hostile to creative work. Paradoxically, universities are among them. One of the main functions of a university is to extend the frontiers of knowledge. Therefore you would expect a university to be a community of creative scientists, engineers, philosophers, historians, economists, psychologists and so on. But academics are selected and promoted mainly on account of their intelligence, even cleverness, as analytical and critical scholars, not as creative thinkers. An over-critical atmosphere can develop. When, as a young historian, G M Trevelyan told his professor that he wanted to write books on history he was at once advised to leave Cambridge University. Iris Murdoch left academic life as a philosopher at Oxford partly for the same reason: writing creative fiction is seldom done well in the critical climate of a university.

The same principle applies to schools, colleges, churches, industrial and commercial organizations, even families. Surround yourself with people who are not going to subject your ideas to premature criticism. 'I can achieve that easily by not talking about them', you might reply. Yes, but that cheats you out of the kinds of discussion that are generally valuable to thinkers. These fall under the general principle that 'two heads are better than one'. It is useful to hear another person's perspective on the problem. They may have relevant experience or knowledge. They are likely to spot and challenge your unconscious assumptions. They can lead you to question your preconceptions and what you believe are facts. In short, you need other people in order to think – for thinking is a social activity – but you do not need over-critical people, or those who cannot reserve their critical responses in order to fit in with your needs.

KEYPOINTS

▪ Suspending judgement means erecting a temporary and artificial barrier between the analysing and synthesizing faculties of your mind on the one hand, and the valuing faculty on the other.

▪ Premature criticism from others can kill off seeds of creative thinking. Besides managing your own critical faculty you have to turn the critical faculties of others to good account. That entails knowing when and how to avoid criticism as well as when and how to invite it.

▪ Some social climates in families, working groups or organizations encourage and stimulate creative thinking, while others stifle or repress it. The latter tend to value analysis and criticism above originality and innovative thinking.

▪ Neither praise nor blame is the object of true criticism. Justly to discriminate, firmly to establish, wisely to prescribe and honestly to be aware – these are the true aims and duties of criticism.

To find fault is easy; to do better may be difficult.
Plutarch

17

Learn to tolerate ambiguity

Chaos often breeds life, when order breeds habit.

Henry Adams

'Negative Capability, that is when a man is capable of being in uncertainties, mysteries, doubts, without any irritable reaching after fact and reason.' These words of the poet John Keats point to an important attribute. It was, he felt, the supreme gift of William Shakespeare as a creative thinker. It is important, he adds, for all creative thinkers to be able 'to remain content with half-knowledge'. Keats's contemporary, Samuel Taylor Coleridge, said much the same. He spoke of 'that willing suspension of belief for the moment, which constitutes poetic faith'.

Some people by temperament find any sort of ambiguity uncomfortable and even stressful. They jump to certainties – any certainties – just to escape from the unpleasant state of not knowing. They are like the young man who will not wait to meet the right girl, however long the waiting, but marries, simply in order to escape from the state of being unmarried.

Thinking sometimes leads you up to a locked door. You are denied entry, however hard you knock. There seems to be some insurmountable barrier, a refusal to give you what you are seeking. Yet you sense something is there. You feel as if you are in a state of suspended animation; you are wandering around in the dark. All you have are unanswered or half-answered questions, doubts, uncertainties and contradictions. You are like a person who suspects there is something gravely wrong with their health and is awaiting the results of medical tests. The temptation to anxiety or fear is over-whelming. Anxiety is diffused fear, for the object of it is not known clearly or visibly. If you are in a jungle and see a tiger coming towards you, you are afraid; if there is no tiger and you still feel afraid, you are suffering from anxiety.

In the health analogy what the person needs is courage. Courage does not mean the absence of anxiety or fear – we would be inhuman not to experience them. It means the ability to contain, control or manage anxiety, so that it does not freeze us into inaction.

More creative thinkers have a higher threshold of tolerance to uncertainty, complexity and apparent disorder than others. For these are conditions that often produce the best results. They do not feel a need to reach out and pluck a premature conclusion or unripe solution. That abstinence requires an intellectual form of courage. For you have to be able to put up with doubt, obscurity and ambiguity for a long time, and these are negative states within the kingdom of the positive.

The negative and the positive are always at each other's throats, so you are condemned to an inner tension.

The great American pioneer Daniel Boone, famous for his journeys into the trackless forests of the Western Frontier in the region we now call Kentucky, was once asked if he was ever lost. 'I can't say I was ever lost,' he replied slowly, after some reflection, 'but I was once sure bewildered for three days.' As a creative thinker you may never feel quite lost, but you will certainly be bewildered for long stretches of time. 'Ambiguity' comes from a Latin verb meaning 'to wander around'. When your mind does not know where it is going, it has to wander around.

Courage and perseverance are cousins. 'I think and think, for months, for years', said Einstein. 'Ninety nine times the conclusion is false. The hundredth time I am right.' Creative thinking often – not always – does require an untiring patience. Secrets are not yielded easily. You have to be willing, if necessary, to persist in your particular enterprise of thought, despite counter-influences, opposition or discouragement.

When you feel that being persistent is a difficult task, think of the bee. A red clover blossom contains less than one-eighth of a grain of sugar: 7,000 grains are required to make 1 pound of honey. A bee, flitting here and there for sweetness, must visit 56,000 clover heads for 1 pound of honey: and there are about 60 flower tubes to each clover head. When a bee performs that operation 60 times 56,000 or 3,360,000 times, it secures enough sweetness for only 1 pound of honey!

KEYPOINTS

▪ Negative Capability is your capacity to live with doubt and uncertainty over a sustained period of time. 'One doesn't discover new lands,' said French novelist, André Gide, 'without consenting to lose sight of the shore for a very long time.'

▪ 'Doubt is not a pleasant mental state,' said Voltaire, 'but certainty is a ridiculous one.'

▪ It is part of a wider tolerance of ambiguity that we all need to develop as people. For life ultimately is not clearly understandable. It is riven with mystery. The area of the inexplicable increases as we grow older.

▪ 'A man without patience is a lamp without oil', said Andrés Segovia. Creative thinking is a form of active, energetic patience. Wait for order to emerge out of chaos. It needs a midwife when its time has come.

▪ 'Take care that the nectar does not remain within you in the same state as when you gathered it', wrote Petrarch. 'Bees would have no credit unless they transformed it into something different and better.'

▪ The last key in the bunch is often the one to open the lock.

There must be a beginning of any great matter, but the continuing unto the end until it be thoroughly finished yields the true glory.

Sir Francis Drake

18

Drift, wait and obey

Day-dreaming is thought's Sabbath.

Amiel

The longer you are in the presence of a difficulty the less likely you are to solve it. Although creative thinking requires sustained attention, sometimes over a period of years, it does not always have to be conscious attention. It is as if you are delegating the question, problem or opportunity to another departure of your mind. Having briefed your Depth Mind, as it were, by conscious mental work, you should then switch off your attention. Wait for your unconscious mind to telephone you: 'Hey, have you thought of this... '

You should learn to expect your Depth Mind to earn its living. Remember that the testimonies to its capacity for creative work are overwhelming. The writer H E Bates said:

> My stories and the people in them are almost wholly bred in imagination, that part of the brain of which we really know so little, their genesis over and over again inspired by little things, a face at a window, a chance remark, the disturbing quality of a pair of eyes, the sound of wind on a seashore. From such apparent trivialities, from the merest grain of fertile seed, do books mysteriously grow.

A friendly and positive expectancy is rewarded when your Depth Mind stirs. The important thing then is not to keep your analytical and critical powers switched off. 'When your daemon is in charge,' said Rudyard Kipling, 'do not try to think consciously. Drift, wait and obey.'

George Benjamin is one of the world's most prominent composers:

> I hate it when people describe my composing as a 'gift'. All people have gifts, even if they don't all realize them. I'm lucky enough to have been encouraged to believe in my abilities. When I'm composing I start slowly. For weeks I don't really do anything, just walk round in circles, thinking. But that is the composition: the mind subconsciously sorts things out, and later on it comes pouring out – as though the piece were writing itself. An orchestral work can contain several hundred thousand notes, all relating to one another. At the beginning one is trying to determine the laws that will govern those relationships, which is intellectual rather than creative. But none of the hard work is wasted. The mind connects things in unbelievable ways. And at the end, it all pours out.

The mind does indeed connect things in unbelievable ways. For Leonardo da Vinci the worlds of science and art were deeply interconnected. His scientific notebooks were filled with pictures, colours and images; his sketchbook for paintings abounded with geometry, anatomy and perspective. He wrote:

To develop a complete mind:
Study the science of art;
Study the art of science.
Learn how to see.
Realize that everything
connects to everything else.

Remember those words of Rodin: 'I invent nothing; I rediscover.' It may help you to have confidence if you know there are connections: then it becomes a matter of discerning, selecting and combining.

You may become aware that your Depth Mind has done some work for you when your body is active but your mind is in neutral. Ideas often come to people when they are walking or driving a car. Both the key connections that led to the development of X-ray crystallography and to the invention of the body scanner occurred to their originators while out walking. Physical relaxation – sitting on a train, having a bath, lying awake in the morning – is another conducive state.

The novelist John le Carré is one of the many creative thinkers who find that walking plays a part in the total economy of creative thinking, albeit not a direct one:

I have a walking appetite just as I have other appetites, and am quite frustrated if it can't be answered on demand. Moving gets me unclogged in my head. I almost never make a note when I'm walking and usually forget the great lines I have composed, which is probably just as well. But I come home knowing that life is possible and even, sometimes, beautiful.

KEYPOINTS

■ Knowing when to turn away from a problem and leave it for a while is an essential skill in the art of creative thinking. It is easier for you to do that if you are confident that your unconscious mind is taking over the baton.

■ Even when ideas – or hints of ideas – are beginning to surface, resist the temptation to start thinking consciously about them. Let them saunter in at their own time and place. A heightened awareness and detached interest on your part will create the right climate.

■ All creative thinking stems from seeing or making connections. Everything is connected with everything else, but our minds cannot always perceive the links.

■ From the myriads of possible combinations, moreover, we have to select according to different criteria according to our field. Is it simple? Is it true? Is it beautiful? Is it useful? Is it practicable? Is it commercial?

■ A person is judged not by his or her answers but by the questions they ask.

To raise new questions, new possibilities, to regard old problems from a new angle, requires creative imagination and marks real advance in science.

Einstein

19

Sleep on the problem

It is the heart always that sees, before the head can see.
Thomas Carlyle

When you are relaxed in bed before going to sleep it is good to think about an issue requiring some Depth Mind activity. The value of doing so has long been known. As Leonardo da Vinci wrote: 'It is no small benefit on finding oneself in bed in the dark to go over again in the imagination the main lines of the forms previously studied, or other noteworthy things conceived by ingenious speculation.'

Of course you might actually dream of a solution. Why we dream is still largely a mystery. Dreams are extraordinary creations of our imagining faculty in the inner brain.

Sometimes they have messages from the hidden parts of our brain for us, not by telephone this time but coded in an alien language of images.

The man who invented the Singer sewing machine reached an impasse when he could not get the thread to run through the needle consistently. When he was at his wit's end he dreamed one night that he was being chased by natives carrying spears. As they came closer, he noticed that every spear had a hole at the bottom of the blade, and the next morning he made a needle with its eye near the point, instead of at the top. His machine was complete.

You may like to try the experiment of jotting down fragments of dreams you can recall when you wake up. See how many suggestions or meanings you can discern in them. Even if they do not solve your problems, dreams may reveal your true feelings and desires, especially if these have been suppressed for too long. As William Golding said, 'Sleep is when all the unsorted stuff comes flying out from a dustbin upset in a high wind.'

Occasionally you will be rewarded by a real clue in your dreams. Roy Plomley on *Desert Island Discs* narrated one such instance involving Sir Basil Spence, the distinguished architect who designed Coventry Cathedral:

> In designing a project of such vast size and complexity there were bound to be snags. He told me that at one point, when he was held up by a particular technical difficulty, he had an abscess on a tooth and went to his dentist, who proposed to remove the molar under a local anaesthetic. As soon as he had the injection, Spence passed out. During the short time he was unconscious he had a very vivid dream of walking through the completed cathedral, with the choir singing and the organ playing, and the sun shining through stained glass

windows towards the altar – and that is the way he subsequently planned it. Another inspiration was received when, flipping though the pages of a natural history magazine, he came across an enlargement of the eye of a fly, and that gave him the general lines for the vault.

The philosopher Thomas Hobbes kept a notebook at hand. 'As soon as a thought darts,' he said, 'I write it down.'

Follow up an idea promptly. Once, when Newton had a particularly illuminating idea while walking down the steps of his wine cellar to fetch a bottle for some guests, he promptly abandoned his errand. The bemused guests discovered him some time later hard at work in his study!

Quite why sleep plays such an important part in helping or enabling the Depth Mind to analyse, synthesize and value is still a mystery. Dreams suggest an inner freedom to make all sorts of random connections between different constellations of brain cells. There may be some sort of shaking up of the kaleidoscope, resulting in new patterns forming in the mine shafts of the mind. We just do not know. This ignorance of *how* the Depth Mind works does not matter very much. What does matter is that it does work. As the Chinese proverb says, 'It does not make any difference if the cat is black or white as long as it catches mice.'

There is an element of mystery about this creative work that can go on in our sleep. Robert Louis Stevenson spoke of 'those little people, my brownies, who do one half my work for me while I am fast asleep, and in all human likelihood do the rest for me as well, when I am wide awake and fondly suppose I do it for myself'.

There are times that do seem conducive to the work of the Depth Mind, times of prolonged solitude, for example, or times when we lie awake in the still of the night, warm and relaxed in bed. 'When I am completely myself,' wrote Mozart to his father, 'entirely alone or during the night when I cannot sleep, it is on these occasions that my ideas flow best and most abundantly. Whence and how these come I know not nor can I force them. Nor do I hear in my imagination the parts successfully, but I hear them at the same time altogether.'

KEYPOINTS

■ You most probably have experienced the beneficial effects of sleeping on a problem, and awakening to find that your mind has made itself up. Use that principle by programming your Depth Mind for a few minutes as you lie in the dark and before you go to sleep.

■ Your dreams may occasionally be directly relevant. It is much more likely, however, that some indication, clue or idea will occur to you after 'sleeping on it'. Perhaps during your waking hours, for instance while you are shaving or washing the dishes, the idea will dart into your mind.

■ Do you remember Francis Bacon's advice? 'A man would do well to carry a pencil in his pocket and write down the thoughts of the moment. Those that come unsought are commonly the most valuable and should be secured, because they seldom return.' Always keep a pad and pencil by your bedside: when a brief idea comes, write it down.

■ Somebody once asked Anton Bruckner: 'Master, how, when, where did you think of the divine motif of your *Ninth Symphony*?' 'Well, it was like this,' Bruckner replied, 'I walked up the Kahlenberg and when it got hot and I got hungry, I sat down by a little brook and unpacked my Swiss cheese. and just as I open the greasy paper that tune pops into my head!'

An idea is a feat of association.

Robert Frost

20

Working it out

There is an old saying 'Well begun is half done.' 'Tis a bad one. I would use instead, 'Not begun at all till half done.'
John Keats

Creative thinking and creativity are not quite the same thing. Creative thinking leads you to the new idea; creativity includes actually bringing it into existence. To give something form – to bring an idea actually into existence – requires a range of skills and knowledge beyond the more cerebral ones we have been considering in this book so far. The artist is an obvious case in point. Leonardo da Vinci may have lain in bed in his darkened chamber going over again in his imagination his observations of the previous day and various ideas 'conceived by ingenious speculation'. But when he awoke next morning and went into his studio he had the skill to make models, draw and paint with a consummate artisanship acquired over a lifetime. He may not have translated all his original ideas into existence – in the cases of the helicopter and submarine the technology was lacking – but he could certainly express his ideas in detailed drawings.

One possible relationship between the two concepts of creative thinking and creativity is suggested by dividing them into two distinct phases: thinking precedes making. But in most instances this separation is entirely arbitrary; it just does not correspond to the facts. There are some cases, indeed, where an idea or concept appears initially in its finished and fully fledged form, but they are the exceptions. What is given is less than that. You have to work it out. In the process of working it out the idea may be developed, adapted or changed, and new ideas or materials will be added to the melting pot. As Sir Hugh Wheldon, the renowned television producer once said in a televised lecture, 'Programmes are made in the making.'

This approach may sound rather untidy, even chaotic. And so it is. It goes against the grain for those who have been indoctrinated to seek finished ideas before going to work. But it adds greatly to the interest and excitement of work if you do not know what is coming next. 'I have never started a poem yet whose end I knew', said Robert Frost. Creative thinking has to be an adventure.

Knowing when to stop thinking and to try working out an idea is an important act of judgement. If you are premature you will waste a lot of time fruitlessly chasing ideas that are not right. But if you have a working clue do not wait too long! John Hunter, the famous British surgeon and physiologist in the 18th century, had considerable influence as a teacher. His most brilliant pupil was Edward Jenner, who had already begun to think that he could prevent smallpox by vaccination. 'Don't think,' Hunter advised, 'try it! Be patient, be accurate!' And the pupil spent many years in painstaking observation. In due course, as we all know, Jenner discovered the smallpox vaccine.

The fact that you are starting the journey with inadequate instructions, as it were, means that you are bound to feel bewildered, confused, even frustrated at times – often for quite long periods. You will be tempted to give up. But it is encouraging to know that even professional creative thinkers go through this dark night of despair.

The author Hammond Innes said that he started work on a novel with little more than a background and a theme, probably an opening scene, perhaps even some idea of the climax:

> But each book is different, something to be wrestled with, struggled over. And there is always the point, somewhere in the writing of it, when all seems hopeless and I am driven to desperation by the thought that I have lost my touch as a story-teller, will never be able to do it again. Blank despair is matched by excitement, the enormous satisfaction when suddenly it all falls into place, seemingly of its own accord, and the words begin to flow again, the whole thing fascinating, totally absorbing.

As Hammond Innes commented, the process sounds more like a battle – at least 50 per cent of his writing output went in the wastepaper basket – than a recipe for success. 'Then why not an outline of the story first?' he was often asked. 'Surely that would be simpler?' He replied, 'Of course it would. But if I did that, then there would be no fun in writing it. And if the writer is bored, then the reader will be even more bored. The story must grow, naturally and of its own volition – a slow, haphazard, infuriating process, but the only one I know.'

Not surprisingly, it took Hammond Innes about four years to produce a book. The novelist John Fowles, author of *The French Lieutenant's Woman*, was equally slow. He worked on several books at once, constantly reworking and rewriting sections of them, beginning one and then moving aside to another. In 10 years, he once said, 'I may have started as many as 12 but only finished three.' Fowles, like Innes, never planned a novel:

> I begin with an image, a ghost of an idea, nothing more, not knowing where it will lead. After about 10,000 to 15,000 words you can tell if it's coming alive, you feel waves – radioactive waves – coming from it. Usually I will write the first 20,000 words in sequence – but after that I may jump ahead, write a later scene, and then go back and fill in. Or turn to something else.

The novels of John Fowles lived with him day in, day out. It is this that perhaps explained his reluctance to publish. 'That is the death-point', he told one interviewer. 'Once the book is handed over, once it's set, then you are locked out from your own text. The joy is in the gathering of the invention, when you have the molten metal, the liquid bronze... when your material seems to have a life of its own. When it's cast...', he broke off and shrugged. The interviewer concluded that Fowles disliked talking about his past books, and he would never discuss those on which he was still working. The one was dying for him, the other being born.

While you are working in this way, ideas arise from within you, you know not where from. Your whole mind is at work, so that you lose consciousness of time and place. The most exciting times are when you are fearful as to what the outcome is going to be: not knowing whether or not it will come off. There is tension. When it stands up and salutes your mind, when it is over and you contemplate it, then there are moments of exaltation. Always there is some sort of excitement. Just being there is exciting.

Creative thinking, then, cannot be divorced from the process of working it out. Because it is part of creative thinking this work has to be done by the person concerned: it cannot be delegated. The playwright must write the script; the composer must compose the score; the inventor must build the model; and the designer must do the sketch or plan. Actors, musicians, craftspeople and technicians will have important roles to play in the total drama of an act of creation. For instance, without a select team of skilled people – typesetter, book designer, printer, binder and bookseller – you would never read the words I am writing now. But such contributions are essentially downstream from the primary activities of having the idea and working it out.

KEYPOINTS

■ Working it out – actually trying to make or produce something – is a way of continuing the process of creative thinking. Therefore it is not necessary to have a fully formed picture, or crystal clear idea of where you are going, before you start work.

■ Because so little is given to you by way of initial inspiration you may follow false trails, get lost and feel frustrated, even to the point of despairing. But if you haven't worked on the edge of failure you haven't worked on the edge of real success.

■ As implementation is part of creative thinking you have to develop the product yourself, at least up to a certain point. Beyond that point it obviously has to be much more of a team effort, especially if you wish to take the idea into the marketplace.

■ Exhilaration is that feeling you get just after a great idea hits you, and just before you realize what's wrong with it.

The creative act thrives in an environment of mutual stimulation, feedback and constructive criticism in a community of creativity.

Anon

21

Think creatively about your life

Creativeness and a creative attitude to life as a whole is not man's right, it is his duty.

Nikolai Berdyaev

Much of this book has been about creative thinking in the context of work. On the assumption that we all have some creative ability I have drawn upon examples of authors and artists, inventors and entrepreneurs, scientists and crafts-people, in order to identify some general principles that are relevant to all of us.

But creative thinking has a more general application. You may not be an author of books, but you are writing the book of your own life. For your life is not being dictated to you from a prerecorded script. You can make at least some of it up as you go along. 'When the creative urge seizes one – at least, such is my experience – one becomes creative in all directions at once', said Henry Miller.

If you decide to take a creative approach to life it does change your perspective. You will seek out first some 'given' ideas about yourself. What are your distinctive strengths? These are not easy questions to answer. Self-discovery lasts a lifetime, and even then it may not be completed. Seek to identify what you are born to excel at, and make sure you are working in the right area.

Even when some conscious self-analysis and some imaginative thinking, supplemented by intuition, have given you some clues, insights or bold guesses about yourself, you still have to try to work out these ideas in a real life. That involves an element of trial – and error – periods of frustration and despair, and moments of excitement and joy.

For gradually, the creative pattern of your life begins to emerge before your eyes on the loom of experience, with change and continuity as its warp and weft. At her 80th birthday celebration the internationally famous weaver Theo Moorman had words to say that apply to our lives as well as our work:

> Set your sights high, otherwise the whole momentum collapses. Cherish your integrity and judgement. You can't work with one eye on the market, you have to stand for yourself. When I take my work off the loom, occasionally there's a comeback feeling in one's gut that tell one it is good. It's a feeling to be prized above rubies.

Life should be an adventure. It is a usually interesting, occasionally exciting and sometimes painful journey forwards into an unknown future. As you try to make something of it in a creative way – working things out as you go along – new ideas will come to you. Even in the desert stretches there are wells and springs of inspiration. But they are not to be had in advance.

A person who thinks creatively will never look upon life as finished. 'I have no objection to retirement,' Mark Twain once said, 'as long as it doesn't interrupt my work.' We can all learn from creative thinkers to see life as essentially a series of beginnings. 'I love beginnings', says novelist Christopher Leach. 'What I like about life is the potentiality of beginnings.' Perhaps our lives, like books, should never be finished, only abandoned to a receiver with as much trust as we can muster.

KEYPOINTS

▪ Even if your work in the narrow sense does not call for imagination, the art of creative thinking is still relevant to you. For our lives are unfinished creations. Shaping and transforming the raw materials of our lives and circumstances is endlessly interesting and often challenging. Almost everything comes from almost nothing.

▪ It is not what happens to you in life that matters but how you respond. The creative response is to transform bad things into good, problems into opportunities.

▪ Remember the Arab proverb, 'You should never finish building your house'. It is beginnings and the unfinished work to be done that excites your creative mind. Endings belong to God. Fortunately for us, they are not our business here on earth.

▪ 'Life is what happens when you are busy making other plans' (John Lennon).

▪ The freedom you give yourself to make mistakes is the best environment for creativity.

If you want to make God smile, tell him your plans.
Spanish proverb

Appendix A

Checklist: Have you analysed the problem?

Understanding the problem

- Have you defined the problem or objective in your own words?

- Are there any other possible definitions of it worth considering? What general solutions do they suggest?

- Decide what you are trying to do. Where are you now and where do you want to get to?

- Identify the important facts and factors. Do you need to spend more time on obtaining more information? What are the relevant policies, rules or procedures?

- Have you reduced the complex problem to its simplest terms without over-simplifying it?

Towards solving the problem

- Have you checked all your main assumptions?

- Ask yourself and others plenty of questions. What? Why? How? When? Where? Who?

- List the obstacles that seem to block your path to a solution.

- Work backwards. Imagine for yourself the end state, and then work from there to where you are now.

- List all the possible solutions, ways forward or courses of action.

- Decide upon the criteria by which they must be evaluated.

- Narrow down the list to the feasible solutions, that is, the ones that are possible given the resources available.

- Select the optimum one, possibly in combination with parts of others.

- Work out an implementation programme complete with dates or times for completion.

Evaluating the solution

- Be sure that you have used all the important information.

- Check your proposed solution from all angles.

- Ensure that the plan is realistic.

- Review the solution or decision in the light of experience.

Appendix B

Checklist: Are you using your Depth Mind?

- Do you have a friendly and positive attitude to your Depth Mind? Do you expect it to work for you?

- Where possible, do you build into your plans time to 'sleep on it', so as to give your Depth Mind an opportunity to contribute?

- Name one idea or intuition that has come to you unexpectedly in the last two weeks.

- What physical activities – such as walking or gardening or driving a car – do you find especially conducive to receiving the results of Depth Mind thinking?

▓ Have you experienced waking up next morning and finding that your unconscious mind has resolved some problem or made some decision for you?

▓ Do you see your Depth Mind as being like a computer? Remember the computing acronym RIRO – Rubbish In, Rubbish Out.

▓ 'Few people think more than two or three times a year', said George Bernard Shaw. 'I have made an international reputation for myself by thinking once or twice a week.' How often do you deliberately seek to employ your Depth Mind to help you to analyse a complex matter, synthesize or restructure materials, or reach value judgements?

▓ How could knowledge of how the Depth Mind works help you in your relations to other people?

▓ Do you keep a notebook or pocket tape recorder at hand to capture fleeting or half-formed ideas?

▓ What other clues have you learnt from experience – clues not indicated in this book – on how to get the best out of your unconscious mind?

Appendix C

Answers to quiz and exercise on pages 10–12 and 63

1. A young English designer named Carwardine approached the firm of Herbert Terry at the beginning of the 1930s with the proposal that they should build a desk light employing the constant-tension jointing principles found in the human arm. The company agreed, and the Anglepoise light was the result. From that time it has been in production, scarcely altered except for details and finishes.

2. Cats eyes in the road.

3. Spitfires.

4. Clarence Birdseye took a vacation in Canada and saw some salmon that had been naturally frozen in ice and then thawed. When they were cooked he noticed how fresh they tasted. He borrowed the idea and the mighty frozen food industry was born.

5. They could have suggested the principle of independent suspension.

6. The burrowing movement of earthworms has suggested a new method of mining, which is now in commercial production.

7. In Edinburgh Botanic Gardens there is a plaque commemorating a flower that inspired the design of the Crystal Palace.

8. Sir Basil Spence, the architect of Coventry Cathedral, was flipping through the pages of a natural history magazine when he came across an enlargement of the eye of a fly, and that gave him the general lines for the vault.

9. Linear motors.

10. Ball-and-socket joints.

11. Magnifying glasses.

12. The arch. Possibly the Eskimos were the first to use the arch in the construction of igloos.

13. Hollow steel cylinders.

14. Levers.

15. Bagpipes.

16. Wind instruments.

Exercise on page 63

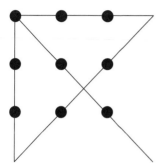

The reason why you may not have been able to solve the problem is that unconsciously your mind imposed a framework around the nine circles. You have to go beyond that invisible box. From this problem, which I introduced in 1969, comes the phrase 'Think outside the box!'

Index